Tucholsky Wagner Zola Scott Sydow Fonatne Freud Schlegel Turgenev Wallace Twain Walther von der Vogelweide Fouqué Friedrich II. von Preußen Freiligrath Weber Frey Kant Ernst Fechner Fichte Weiße Rose von Fallersleben Richthofen Frommel Hölderlin Engels Fielding Eichendorff Tacitus Dumas Fehrs Faber Flaubert Eliasberg Ebner Eschenbach Maximilian I. von Habsburg Fock Zweig Feuerbach Eliot Ewald Vergil Goethe London Elisabeth von Österreich Mendelssohn Balzac Shakespeare Dostojewski Ganghofer Lichtenberg Rathenau Trackl Stevenson Doyle Gjellerup Hambruch Tolstoi Mommsen Lenz Droste-Hülshoff Thoma Hanrieder von Arnim Dach Verne Hägele Hauff Humboldt Reuter Karrillon Rousseau Hagen Hauptmann Garschin Gautier Defoe Baudelaire Damaschke Hebbel Descartes Hegel Kussmaul Herder Wolfram von Eschenbach Schopenhauer Dickens Darwin Rilke George Bronner Melville Grimm Jerome Bebel Campe Horváth Aristoteles Proust Voltaire Federer Bismarck Vigny Barlach Herodot Gengenbach Heine Storm Casanova Tersteegen Grillparzer Georgy Gilm Lessing Chamberlain Langbein Gryphius Brentano Lafontaine Strachwitz Claudius Schiller Kralik Iffland Sokrates Schilling Bellamy Katharina II. von Rußland Raabe Gerstäcker Gibbon Tschechow Löns Hesse Hoffmann Gogol Wilde Vulpius Gleim Luther Heym Hofmannsthal Morgenstern Klee Hölty Goedicke Roth Heyse Klopstock Kleist Luxemburg Puschkin Homer Mörike La Roche Horaz Musil Machiavelli Kierkegaard Kraft Kraus Navarra Aurel Musset Lamprecht Kind Moltke Kirchhoff Hugo Nestroy Marie de France Laotse Ipsen Liebknecht Nietzsche Nansen Marx Ringelnatz Lassalle Gorki Klett von Ossietzky Leibniz May vom Stein Lawrence Irving Petalozzi Platon Knigge Pückler Michelangelo Kafka Sachs Poe Kock Liebermann Korolenko de Sade Praetorius Mistral Zetkin

Hammersmith, Fulham and Putney The Fascination of London

G. E. (Geraldine Edith) Mitton

Imprint

This book is part of the TREDITION CLASSICS series.

Author: G. E. (Geraldine Edith) Mitton
Cover design: toepferschumann, Berlin (Germany)

Publisher: tredition GmbH, Hamburg (Germany)
ISBN: 978-3-8491-8549-7

www.tredition.com
www.tredition.de

The intention of the TREDITION CLASSICS series is to make world literature in the public domain available in printed format. Literary enthusiasts and organizations worldwide have scanned and digitally edited the original texts. tredition has subsequently formatted and redesigned the content into a modern reading layout. Therefore, we cannot guarantee the exact reproduction of the original format of a particular historic edition. Please also note that no modifications have been made to the spelling, therefore it may differ from the orthography used today.

THE FASCINATION
OF LONDON
HAMMERSMITH
WALTER
BESANT

THE FASCINATION

FULHAM PALACE.

The Fascination of London

HAMMERSMITH, FULHAM AND PUTNEY

BY
G. E. MITTON
AND
J. C. GEIKIE

EDITED BY
SIR WALTER BESANT

LONDON
ADAM & CHARLES BLACK
1903

PREFATORY NOTE

A survey of London, a record of the greatest of all cities, that should preserve her history, her historical and literary associations, her mighty buildings, past and present, a book that should comprise all that Londoners love, all that they ought to know of their heritage from the past—this was the work on which Sir Walter Besant was engaged when he died.

As he himself said of it: "This work fascinates me more than anything else I've ever done. Nothing at all like it has ever been attempted before. I've been walking about London for the last thirty years, and I find something fresh in it every day."

Sir Walter's idea was that two of the volumes of his survey should contain a regular and systematic perambulation of London by different persons, so that the history of each parish should be complete in itself. This was a very original feature in the great scheme, and one in which he took the keenest interest. Enough has been [Pg viii] done of this section to warrant its issue in the form originally intended, but in the meantime it is proposed to select some of the most interesting of the districts and publish them as a series of booklets, attractive alike to the local inhabitant and the student of London, because much of the interest and the history of London lie in these street associations.

The difficulty of finding a general title for the series was very great, for the title desired was one that would express concisely the undying charm of London—that is to say, the continuity of her past history with the present times. In streets and stones, in names and palaces, her history is written for those who can read it, and the object of the series is to bring forward these associations, and to make them plain. The solution of the difficulty was found in the words of the man who loved London and planned the great scheme. The work "fascinated" him, and it was because of these associations that it did so. These links between past and present in themselves largely constitute The Fascination of London.

G. E. M.
[Pg 1]

HAMMERSMITH

The parish of Hammersmith is mentioned in Doomsday Book under the name of Hermoderwode, and in ancient deeds of the Exchequer as Hermoderworth. It is called Hamersmith in the Court Rolls of the beginning of Henry VII.'s reign. This is evidently more correct than the present spelling of the name, which is undoubtedly derived from *Ham,* meaning in Saxon a town or dwelling, and *Hythe* or *Hyde,* a haven or harbour, "therefore," says Faulkner, "Hamhythe, a town with a harbour or creek."

Hammersmith is bounded on the south by Fulham and the river, on the west by Chiswick and Acton, and on the east by Kensington. Until 1834 it was incorporated with the parish of Fulham, and on Ascension Day of that year the first ceremony of "beating the bounds" took place. The West London Railway runs in the bed of an ancient stream which rose north of Wormwood Scrubs and ended at Chelsea Creek, and this brook was crossed by a bridge at the [Pg 2] place where the railway-bridge now stands on the Hammersmith Road. The stream was evidently the determining factor in the old parish boundary line between Kensington and Hammersmith, but Hammersmith borough includes this, ending at Norland and St. Ann's Roads. On the south side it marches with Fulham—that is to say, westward along the Hammersmith Road as far as St. Paul's School, where it dips southward to include the school, and thence to the river. From here it proceeds midway in the river to a point almost opposite the end of Chiswick Ait, then northward up British Grove as far as Ravenscourt Gardens; almost due north to within a few yards of the Stamford Brook Road; it follows the trend of that road to the North and South Western Junction Railway. It crosses the railway three times before going northward until it is on a level with Jeddo Road. It then turns eastward, cuts across the north of Jeddo Road to Wilton Road West. Northward it runs to the Uxbridge Road, follows this eastward for a few yards, and strikes again northward up Old Oak Road and Old Oak Common Road until it reaches Wormwood Scrubs public and military ground. It then trends north-eastward, curves back to meet the Midland and South-Western Line as it crosses the canal, and follows Old Oak Common Road until on a level with Willesden Junction Station, from thence [Pg 3] eastward to the Harrow Road. It follows the Harrow Road until it meets the western Kensington boundary running between the Roman Catholic and Protestant cemeteries at Kensal Town. It goes through Brewster Gardens and Latimer Road until it meets the line first indicated.

HISTORY.

With Fulham, Hammersmith shared in the incursion of the Danes in 879, and it is especially mentioned in the Chronicle of Roger de Hoveden that they wintered in the island of Hame, which Faulkner thinks is the ait or island near Chiswick, which, he says, must have considerably decreased in size during the nine centuries that have elapsed. In 1647 Cromwell removed his quarters from Isleworth to Hammersmith, and "when he was at Sir Nicholas Crispe's house, the headquarters were near the church." The general officers were quartered at Butterwick, now Bradmore House, then the property of the Earl of Mulgrave.

Perambulation.—The first thing noticeable after crossing the boundary from Kensington is St. Paul's School. It stands on the south side of the road, an imposing mass of fiery red brick in an ornamental style. The present building was erected in 1884 by Alfred Waterhouse, and a [Pg 4] statue to the memory of Dean Colet, the founder, standing within the grounds was unveiled in 1902. It was designed by W. Hamo Thornycroft, R.A. The frontage of the building measures 350 feet, and the grounds, including the site, cover six acres. Dr. John Colet, D.D., Dean of St. Paul's, founded his school in 1509 in St. Paul's Churchyard, but it is not known how far he incorporated with it the then existing choir-school. The number of his pupils was 153, in accordance with the number of fishes in the miraculous draught, and the foundation scholars are limited to the same number at the present day. The old school stood on the east side of St. Paul's Churchyard, and suffered so much in the Great Fire that it had to be completely rebuilt. When, in the nineteenth century, the site had become very valuable, the school was removed to Hammersmith, and its original site is now covered by business premises. Dean Colet endowed the foundation by leaving to it lands that were estimated by Stow to be worth £120 annually, and that are now valued at over £20,000. The school is governed under a scheme framed by the Charity Commissioners in 1900, and part of the income is diverted to maintain the new girls' school in Brook Green.

Lily, the grammarian, was the first headmaster, and the roll of the pupils includes many great [Pg 5] names—the antiquaries Leland, Camden, and Strype; John Milton, prince of poets; Halley, the astronomer; Samuel Pepys; Sir Philip Francis, supposed author of the "Letters of Junius"; the famous Duke of Marlborough; among Bishops, Cumberland, Fisher, Ollivant and Lee; among statesmen, Charles, Duke of Manchester, Spencer Compton (Earl of Wilmington), Prime Minister; and Lord Chancellor Truro; also Sir Frederick Pollock, Lord Hannen, Sir Frederick Halliday, and Benjamin Jowett.

The preparatory school, called Colet Court, stands opposite on the northern side of the road. It was founded in 1881, and owns two and a half acres of land. On the same side Kensington Co-operative Stores covers the site of White Cottage, for some time the residence of Charles Keene.

Next to the Red Cow public-house lived Dr. Burney, D.D., LL.D., learned father of a celebrated daughter, who became afterwards Madame D'Arblay. He kept a school here for seven years from 1786. There are other old houses in the vicinity, but to none of them is there attached any special interest. The Convent of the Poor Sisters of Nazareth is in a large brick building on the south side of the road. This was built in 1857 for the convent purposes. It is the mother-house of the Nazareth nuns, so that the [Pg 6] numbers continually vary, many passing through for their noviciate. The nuns collect alms for the aged poor and children, and many of the poor are thus sustained. Besides this, there are a number of imbecile or paralytic children who live permanently in the convent. The charity is not confined to Roman Catholics.

The Latymer Foundation School is a plain brick building standing a little back from the highroad. It bears the Latymer arms, and a cross in stone over the doorway, as well as the date of the foundation. The Latymer charity was established in 1824 by the will of Edward Latymer. He left several pieces of land in the hands of trustees, who were to apply the rents to the following uses:

"To elect and choose eight poor boys inhabiting Hammersmith within the age of twelve and above the age of seven, and provide for every boy a doublet and a pair of breeches of frieze or leather, one shirt, one pair of stockings, and a pair of shoes on the 1st of November; and also to provide yearly, against Ascension Day, a doublet and a pair of breeches of coarse canvas lined, and deliver the same unto the said boys, and also a shirt, one pair of stockings, and a pair of shoes; and that on the left sleeve of every poor boy's doublet a cross of red cloth or baize should be fastened and worn; and that the feofees should cause the boys to be put to some petty school to learn to read English till they attain thirteen, and to instruct them in some part of God's true religion. The allowance of clothing to cease at thirteen. And that the feofees shall also elect six poor aged men of honest conversation inhabiting Hammersmith, and provide for every one of them coats or cassocks of frieze or cloth, and deliver the same upon the 1st of November in every year, a cross of red [Pg 7] cloth or baize to be fastened on the left sleeve; and that yearly, on Ascension Day, the feofees should pay to each man ten shillings in money."

To this charity were added various sums from benefactors from time to time, and the number of recipients was increased gradually, until in 1855 there were 100 boys and 45 almsmen. At that date the men's clothing consisted of a body coat, breeches, waistcoat, hat, pair of boots, stockings, and shirt one year, and the next, great-coat, breeches, pair of boots, stockings, shirt, and hat. The boys received coat, waistcoat, and trousers, cap, pair of stockings, shirt, pair of bands, pair of boots. Also on November 1, cap, pair of stockings, shirt, pair of bands, and pair of boots. At present part of the money is given in alms, and the rest is devoted to the Lower Latymer School and the Upper Latymer School, built 1894, situated in King Street West.

At the back of the Latymer Foundation, in Great Church Lane, is the Female Philanthropic Society. The object is for the reformation of young women convicted for a first offence or addicted to petty pilfering.

Opposite is a recreation-ground and St. Paul's parochial room, a small temporary iron building. In King's Mews, Great Church Lane, Cipriani, the historical painter and engraver, lived at one time. He died here in 1785. The entrance to [Pg 8] Bradmore House, the oldest house in Hammersmith, is in the lane. The grounds stretch out a long way eastward, and one or two old cedars are still growing here. The eastern portion of the house has a fine front with fluted pilasters, with Ionic capitals running up to a stone parapet surmounted by urns. The windows are circular-headed, and those over the central doorway belong to a great room, 30 feet by 20, and 20 in height. The house, though much altered, is in its origin part of a very old building named Butterwick House, built by Edmund, third Baron Sheffield and Earl of Mulgrave, about the latter end of Queen Elizabeth's reign. The name was taken from a village in Lincolnshire where the Sheffield family had long lived. This Earl of Mulgrave was grandfather of John, Duke of Buckingham. He died in 1646, and is buried in the church. The estate probably passed from the Sheffield family soon after his death, for in 1653 the manor-house or farm of Butterwick, called the Great House, "passed to Margaret Clapham, wife of Christopher Clapham and widow of Robert Moyle, and her son Walter Moyle after her." In 1677 it was conveyed by Walter Moyle for the use of Anne Cleeve and her heirs. She aliened it to Mr. Ferne in 1700. The house was greatly modernized by Mr. Ferne, Receiver-General of the Customs, who added some rooms to the north-east, "much [Pg 9] admired," says Lysons, "for their architectural beauty."

He intended this part of the house for Mrs. Oldfield, the actress, but she never inhabited it. One of Mr. Ferne's daughters married a Mr. Turner, who in 1736 sold the house to Elijah Impey, father of Sir Elijah Impey, Chief Justice of Bengal. He divided the modern part built by Mr. Ferne from the older building, and called it Bradmore House, and under this name it was used as a school for more than a century. It was again divided into two parts, and the western portion, which fronts the church, is of dark brick with red-brick facings, which glow through the overhanging creepers.

The older part was sold by the Impey family in 1821, and fifteen years later was pulled down. Some small houses, which still stand on the south side, with irregular tiled roofs and walls covered with heavy green ivy, were built on the site. St. Paul's Church, the foundation-stone of which was laid July, 1882, by the late Duke of Albany, is opposite. The square pinnacled tower rises to a considerable height. The original structure was much more ancient. Bowack says:

"The limits of this chapel was divided from Fulham before the year 1622, as appears in a benefaction to the poor of Fulham."

The chapel of ease to the parish of Fulham was [Pg 10] founded in 1628, and opened in 1631. The whole cost was about £2,000, of which Sir Nicholas Crispe gave £700. This church was the last consecrated by Archbishop Laud. The old monumental tablets have been carefully preserved, and hang on the walls of the present building. The most important object in the church is a bronze bust of Charles I. on a pedestal 8 or 9 feet high, of black and white marble. Beneath the bust is the inscription:

"This effigies was erected by special appointment of Sir Nicholas Crispe, knight and Baronet, as a grateful commemoration of that glorious Martyr Kinge Charles I. of blessed Memory."

Below, on a pedestal of black marble, is an urn containing the heart of the loyal subject, and on the pedestal beneath is written:

"Within this Urne is entombed the heart of Sir Nicholas Crispe, knight and Baronet, a Loyall sharer in yhe sufferings of his Late and Present Majesty. Hee first setled the Trade of Gould from Guyny, and there built the Castle of Cormantine. Died 25 Feb. 1665 aged 67 years."

Sir Nicholas Crispe's name is closely identified with Hammersmith. He was born in 1598, the son of a London merchant, and, though inheriting a considerable fortune, he was bred up to business. He was subsequently knighted by King Charles I., [Pg 11] and made one of the farmers of the King's Customs. During the whole of the Civil War he never faltered from his allegiance, but raised money and carried supplies to the King constantly. He had built Brandenburg House (p. 39), on which he is said to have spent £23,000. This was confiscated by Cromwell and used by his troops during the rebellion, but at the Restoration Sir Nicholas was reinstated and rewarded by a baronetcy. His body was not buried at Hammersmith, but in the church of St. Mildred in Bread Street with his ancestors. There is a portrait of him given in Lysons' "Environs of London." He is "said to have been the inventor of the art of making bricks as now practised" (Lysons). He left £100 for the poor of Hammersmith, to be distributed as his trustees and executors should think fit. This amount, being expended in land and buildings, has enormously increased in value, and at the present day brings in a yearly income of £52 15s. 5d., which is spent on blankets for the poor inhabitants of the parish. The only other monuments worthy of notice in the church are those of Edmund, Lord Sheffield, Earl of Mulgrave and Baron of Butterwick, who died 1646; one of the Impey monuments, which hangs over the north door, which contains no less than nine names, and another on the wall close by, to the memory of Sir Elijah Impey and his wife, who are [Pg 12] both buried in the family vault beneath the church. These are plain white marble slabs surmounted by coats of arms.

There is a monument to W. Tierney Clarke, C.E., F.R.S., who designed the suspension-bridge at Hammersmith and executed many other great engineering designs; also a monument to Sophia Charlotte, widow of Lord Robert Fitzgerald, son of James, Duke of Leinster.

These are all on the north wall, and are very much alike.

On the south aisle hangs a plain, unpretentious little slab of marble to the memory of Thomas Worlidge, artist and engraver, who died 1766. His London house was in Great Queen Street, and in it he had been preceded by Kneller and Reynolds, but in his last years he spent much time at his "country house" at Hammersmith. Not far off is the name of Arthur Murphy, barrister and dramatic writer, died 1805. Above the south door is a monument of Sir Edward Nevill, Justice of the Common Pleas, died 1705. In the baptistery at the west end stands a beautiful font cut from a block of white veined marble. In the churchyard rows of the old tombstones, which were displaced when the new church was built, stand against the walls of the adjacent school. Adjoining the churchyard on the south there once stood Lucy House, for many generations the home of the [Pg 13] Lucys, descendants of the justice who prosecuted Shakespeare for deer-stealing.

In the churchyard stand the schools, formerly the Latymer and Charity Schools, now merely St. Paul's National Schools. The school was originally built in 1756 at the joint expense of the feofees of Mr. Latymer and trustees of the Female Charity School, and was restored and added to in 1814. The Charity School was founded in

1712 by Thomas Gouge, who left £50 for the purpose, which has since been increased by other benefactions.

On the south side of the church are two picturesque old cottages, which would seem to be contemporary with the old church itself. Near the north end of the Fulham Palace Road, which here branches off from Queen Street, is the Roman Catholic Convent of the Good Shepherd. The walls enclose nine acres of ground, part of which forms a good-sized garden at the back. The nucleus of the nunnery was a private house called Beauchamp House. The convent is a refuge for penitents, of whom some 230 are received. These girls contribute to their own support by laundry and needle work.

Chancellor Road is so called through having been made through the grounds of an old house of that name. In St. James Street there is a small mission church, called St. Mark's, attended [Pg 14] by the clergy of St. Paul's. In Queen Street, which runs from the church down to the river, there are one or two red-tiled houses, but toward the river end it is squalid and miserable. Bowack says that in his time (1705) two rows of buildings ran from the chapel riverwards, and another along the river westward to Chiswick. One of the first two is undoubtedly Queen Street. The last is the Lower Mall, in which there are several old houses, including the Vicarage, but there is no special history attached to any of them. In 1684 a celebrated engineer, Sir Samuel Morland, came to live in the Lower Mall. Evelyn records a visit to him as follows:

"*25th October, 1695.*

"The Abp and myselfe went to Hammersmith, to visite Sir Sam Morland, who was entirely blind, a very mortifying sight. He showed us his invention of writing, which was very ingenious; also his wooden Kalendar, which instructed him all by feeling, and other pretty and useful inventions of mills, pumps, etc."

Sir Samuel was the inventor of the speaking-trumpet, and also greatly improved the capstan and other instruments. He owed his baronetcy to King Charles II., and was one of the gentlemen of the Privy Chamber and Master of Mechanics. He died in 1696, and was buried at Hammersmith. There are here also large lead-mills. Behind the Lower Mall is a narrow passage, called Ashen Place; here is a row of neat brick cottages, [Pg 15] erected in 1868. These were founded in 1865, and are known as William Smith's Almshouses. Besides the building, an endowment of £8,000 in Consols was left by the founder. There are ten inmates, who may be of either sex, and who receive 7s. a week each.

Waterloo Street was formerly Plough and Harrow Lane. Faulkner mentions a Wesleyan Methodist Chapel here, built in 1809, which probably gave its name to Chapel Street hard by.

Near the west end of the Lower Mall is the Friends' Meeting House, a small brick building which, though new, inherits an old tradition; for there is said to have been a meeting-house here from the beginning of the seventeenth century, and one of the meetings was disturbed and broken up by Cromwell's soldiers. At the back is a small burial-ground, in which the earliest stone bears date 1795.

The Lower is divided from the Upper Mall by a muddy creek. This creek can now be traced inland only so far as King Street, but old maps show it to have risen at West Acton. An old wooden bridge, erected by Bishop Sherlock in 1751, crosses it; this is made entirely of oak, and was repaired in 1837 by Bishop Blomfield. Near the creek the houses are poor and mean, inhabited by river-men, etc., and the place is called Little Wapping. There is a little passage between creek [Pg 16] and river, and in it is a low door marked "The Seasons." It was here that Thompson wrote his great poem, in a room overlooking the water, in the upper part of the Doves public-house, which was then a coffee-tavern. The poem was so little appreciated by the booksellers, who then combined the functions of publishers with their own trade, that it was with difficulty he persuaded one of them to give him three guineas for it.

Opposite is Sussex Lodge, once the residence of the Duke of Sussex, who came to the riverside for change of air. It was afterwards inhabited by Captain Marryat, the novelist. Sir Godfrey Kneller lived for a time in the Upper Mall; and Bowack tells us that "Queen Katherine, when Queen-Dowager, kept her palace in the summer time" by the river. This was Catherine of Braganza, consort of Charles II. She came here after his death, and remained until 1692. She took great interest in gardening, and the elms by the riverside are supposed to have been of her planting. Her banqueting-hall survived until within the last thirty years. It was a building with handsome recesses on the front filled by figures cast in lead. In the reign of Queen Anne the celebrated physician Dr. Radcliffe lived in the same house. He had the project of founding a hospital, and began to build, but never carried his intention into effect. He bequeathed the greater part of [Pg 17] his property and his library to the University of Oxford, and was the founder of the famous Radcliffe Library there. Bishop Lloyd of Norwich was a near neighbour at Hammersmith. He died in the Upper Mall in 1710, and left many valuable books to St. John's College, Cambridge.

In Kelmscott House, No. 26, lived William Morris, R.A., whose influence on the artistic development of printing and in many other directions is well known. On a small outer building of the house is a tablet stating that in this house Sir Francis Ronald, F.R.S., made the first electric telegraph, eight miles long, in 1816. Turner, R.A., lived in the Upper Mall, 1808-14, after which he moved to Sandycombe Lodge, Twickenham. After Riverscourt Road there is a hoarding, behind which was Queen Catherine of Braganza's mansion already referred to. Mickephor Alphery, a member of the Russian Imperial Family, took Holy Orders in England in 1618, and lived at Hammersmith. Weltje Street was named after a favourite cook of George IV.'s, who had a house on its site. He is buried in the churchyard. Linden House is old, but has no history. Beavor Lodge, which gives its name to Beavor Lane, was formerly owned by Sir Thomas Beavor. In it now lives Sir W. B. Richmond, K.C.B., R.A. Old Ship Lane takes its name from a picturesque old tavern, the Old Ship, the doorway of which [Pg 18] is still standing. Hammersmith Terrace runs from Black Lion Lane to Chiswick Hall. In it are many old houses remaining. In No. 13 lived P. J. de Loutherbourgh, an artist and member of the Royal Academy. He died here in 1812. Arthur Murphy, whose monument in the church has been mentioned, lived at No. 17. He wrote lives of Fielding, Johnson, and Garrick, besides numerous essays and plays, and was well known to his own contemporaries. Mrs. Mountain, the celebrated singer, also had a house in the terrace.

The fisheries of Hammersmith were formerly much celebrated. They were leased in the seventeenth century to Sir Nicholas Crispe, Sir Abraham Dawes, and others for the value of three salmon annually. Flounders, smelt, salmon, barbel, eels, roach, dace, lamprey, were caught in the river, but even in 1839 fish were growing very scarce. Faulkner, writing at that period, says it was ten years since a salmon had been caught.

In Black Lion Lane is St. Peter's Church, built in 1829. It is of brick, and has a high lantern tower and massive portico, supported by pillars. Close by are the girls' and infant schools, built 1849-52. From this point to the western boundary of the parish there is nothing further of interest.

In King Street West, after No. 229, there is a Methodist Chapel, with an ornamental porch. A few doors westward are the new or Upper Latymer [Pg 19] Schools, with the arms of the founder over the doorway. The buildings are in red brick, with stone facings.

Returning to the north side of the Hammersmith Road, which has for some time been overlooked, we find the King's Theatre, stone-fronted and new, bearing date 1902. Near it is the West London Hospital, instituted May, 1856, and opened in July of the same year. Since that time it has been greatly enlarged, and an immense new wing overlooking Wolverton Gardens has been added. The hospital was incorporated by royal charter, November 1, 1894. It is entirely supported by voluntary contributions.

Near the Broadway is the Convent of the Sacred Heart, standing on ground which has long been consecrated to religious uses, for a nunnery is said to have existed here before the Reformation. In 1669 a Roman Catholic school for girls was founded here, and in 1797 the Benedictine nuns, driven out of France, took refuge in it. The present buildings were erected in 1876 for a seminary, and it was not until 1893 that the nuns of the Sacred Heart re-established a convent within the walls. The present community employ themselves in teaching, and superintend schools of three grades.

There stood in the Broadway until within recent years a charming old building called The Cottage [Pg 20] —one of those picturesque but obstructive details in which our ancestors delighted. Behind the Congregational Chapel there is an old hall, used as a lecture-hall, which was originally a chapel, and which is said by Faulkner to be the oldest place of worship in Hammersmith. It was built by the Presbyterians. The first authentic mention of its minister is in 1700, when the Rev. Samuel Evans "collected on the brief for Torrington at a meeting of Protestant Dissenters held at the White Hart, Hammersmith, 13s. 6d."

In the Brook Green Road Nos. 41 to 45 contain an orphanage called St. Mary's Catholic Orphanage for Girls. On Brook Green itself one or two old cottages with tiled roofs are still to be seen—reminiscences of old Hammersmith. The long strip of grass, in shape like a curving tongue, justifies the name of "Green." Dr. Iles' almshouses, known as the Brook Green Almshouses, have long been established here, though the present buildings date only from 1839. They stand at the corner of Rowan Road, and are rather ornately built in brick with diamond-paned windows. The charity was founded in 1635 by Dr. Iles, who left "houses, almshouses, and land on Brook Green, and moiety of a house in London." The old almshouses were pulled down in 1839. At the north end of Brook Green, next door to the Jolly Gardeners public-house, stood [Pg 21] Eagle House, a very fine old mansion, only demolished within the last twenty years. Bute House stands on the site. Eagle House was built in the style of Queen Anne's reign, and had a fine gateway with two stone piers surmounted by eagles. The back of the house was of wood, and the front of brick, and there was a massy old oak staircase. Like many other old houses, it became for a time a school.

Sion House is a square stuccoed building, plain and without decoration either interior or exterior. This was used as a nunnery until about three years ago, and the wall decorations in the room used by the nuns as a chapel are still quite fresh. This room is ugly and meagre, and without attractiveness. It has a fine garden at the back, stretching out parallel to that of its neighbour, and the two together embrace an area of close upon four acres, which will make a fine playground for the projected school. These gardens are at present neglected tangles of evergreen creepers and trees, but with a little care might be admirably laid out. On Brook Green is now established St. Paul's School for girls, a companion to the large school for boys already described. This is likely to be a very popular institution.

Near the corner of Caithness Road is the Hammersmith and West Kensington Synagogue, opened on September 7, 1890, which forms one [Pg 22] of the thirteen synagogues in London that constitute together the United Synagogue, of which Lord Rothschild is the President. The building was designed by Mr. Delissa Joseph, F.R.I.B.A. The leading features of the design are a gabled façade with sham minarets, and a recessed porch with overhanging balcony. The façade is flanked by square towers containing the staircases.

At the south end of the Green there is quite a Roman Catholic colony. The Almshouses stand on the west side, facing the road, behind a quadrangle of green grass. They were founded in 1824, and contain accommodation for thirty inmates of either sex. Five of the houses are endowed, and the pensioners pass on in rotation from the unendowed to the endowed rooms. They must be Roman Catholics and exceed the age of sixty years before they are received. On the north side of the quadrangle is the Roman Catholic parish church, a fine building in the Gothic style, with a high spire and moulded entrance doorway, built in 1851.

Immediately opposite, across the road, is St. Mary's Training College for elementary school masters. These young men must have passed the King's Scholarship examination and be over the age of eighteen before they enter on the two years' course of study. The large building near on the north side is the practising-school, [Pg 23] where the students learn the art of teaching practically. There is a pretty little chapel in the college, and the walls enclose three acres of land, including site.

St. Joseph's School for pauper children is adjacent to the practising-school, on the north side. This building is certified for 180 children, who are received from the workhouse, etc. They enter at the age of three years, and leave at sixteen for situations. It was founded and is managed by the Daughters of the Cross, and was established in its present quarters September 19, 1892. Faulkner says of Brook Green, "Here is a Roman Catholic Chapel and School called the Arke," so that this part of Hammersmith has long been connected with the Catholics.

In the Blythe Road, No. 79, is a fine old house with an imposing portico, which now overlooks a dingy yard. This is Blythe House, "reported to have been haunted, and many strange stories were reported of ghosts and apparitions having been seen here; but it turned out at last that a gang of smugglers had taken up their residence in it." It was once used as a school, and later on as a reformatory. It is now in the possession of the Swan Laundry Company.

In Blythe Road there is a small mission church called Christ Church. In Shepherd's Bush Road, at the corner of Netherwood Road, is West Ken [Pg 24] sington Park Chapel of the Wesleyan Methodists. Shepherd's Bush and many of the adjoining roads are thickly lined with bushy young plane-trees. St. Simon's Church, in Minford Gardens, is an ugly red-brick building with ornamental facings of red brick, and a high steeple of the same materials. It was built in 1879. St. Matthew's, in Sinclair Road, is very similar, but has a bell-gable instead of a steeple. The foundation-stone was laid 1870. In Ceylon Road there is a Board school. Facing Addison Road Station is the well-known place of entertainment called Olympia, with walls of red brick and stone and a semicircular glass roof. It contains the largest covered arena in London.

Returning once more to the Broadway, we traverse King Street, which is the High Street of Hammersmith. It is very narrow, and, further, blocked by costers' barrows, so that on Saturday nights it is hard work to get through it at all. The pressure is increased by the electric trams, which run on a single set of rails to the Broadway. In King Street is the Hammersmith Theatre of Varieties, the West End Lecture-Hall, and the West End Chapel, held by the Baptists. It stands on the site of an older chapel, which was first used for services of the Church of England, and was acquired by the Baptists in 1793. The old tombstones standing round the present building are memorials of the former burial- [Pg 25] ground. At the west end of King Street is an entrance to Ravenscourt Park, acquired by the L.C.C. in 1888-90. The grounds cover between thirty and forty acres, and are well laid out in flower-beds, etc., at the southern end. The Ravenscourt Park Railway-station is on the east side, and the arched railway-bridge crosses the southern end of the park. A beautiful avenue of fine old elms leads to the Public Library, which is at the north end in what was once the old manor-house.

All this part of Hammersmith was formerly included in the Manor of Pallenswick or Paddingswick. Faulkner says this manor is situated "at Pallengswick or Turnham Green, and extends to the western road." The first record of it is at the end of Edward III.'s reign, when it was granted to Alice Perrers or Pierce, who was one of the King's favourites. She afterwards married Lord Windsor, a Baron, and Lieutenant of Ireland. Report has also declared that King Edward used the manor-house as a hunting-seat, and his arms, richly carved in wood, stood in a large upper room until a few years before 1813. But the house itself cannot have been very ancient then, for Lysons says it had only recently been rebuilt at the date he wrote—namely, 1795. The influence of Alice Perrers over the King was resented by his courtiers, who procured her banishment [Pg 26] when he died in 1378. After her marriage, however, King Richard II. granted the manor to her husband.

There is a gap in the records of the manor subsequently until John Payne died, leaving it to his son William in 1572. This was the "William Payne of Pallenswick, Esq.," who placed a monument in Fulham Church to the memory of himself and his wife before his own death, and who left an island called Makenshawe "to the use of the poor of this parish on the Hammersmith side." This bequest is otherwise described as being part of an island or twig-ait called Mattingshawe, situated in the parish of Richmond in the county of Surrey. At the time the bequest was left the rent-charge on the island amounted to £3 yearly, which was to be distributed among twelve poor men and women the first year, and to be used for apprenticing a poor boy the second year, alternately. Sir Richard Gurney, Lord Mayor of London, bought the manor in 1631. It was several times sold and resold, and in Faulkner's time belonged to one George Scott. It had only then recently begun to be known as Ravenscourt. The house was granted to the commissioners of the public library by the London County Council at a nominal rent, and the library was opened by Sir John Lubbock, March 19, 1890. In a case at the head of the stairs are a series of the Kelmscott [Pg 27] Press books, presented by Sir William Morris. Round the walls of the rooms hang many interesting old prints, illustrative of ancient houses in Hammersmith and Fulham. There is also a valuable collection of cuttings, prints, and bills relating to the local history of the parish. In the entrance hall are hung prints of Rocque's and other maps of Hammersmith, and the original document signed by the enrolled band of volunteers in 1803. Among the treasures of the library may be mentioned the minute-book of the volunteers, a copy of

Bowack's "Middlesex," and an original edition of Rocque's maps of London and environs.

Just outside the park, on the east side, is the Church of Holy Innocents, opposite St. Peter's Schools. It is a high brick building, opened September 25, 1890. There is a Primitive Methodist chapel with school attached in Dalling Road near by. In Glenthorne Road is the Church of St. John the Evangelist, founded in 1858, and designed by Mr. Butterfield. A magnificent organ was built in it by one of the parishioners in memory of her late husband.

Behind the church are the Godolphin Schools, founded in the sixteenth century by the will of W. Godolphin, and rebuilt in 1861. In Southerton Road there is a small Welsh chapel. The Goldhawk Road is an old Roman road, a fact which was conclusively proved by the discovery of the [Pg 28] old Roman causeway accidentally dug up by workmen in 1834.

Shepherd's Bush Green is a triangular piece of grass an acre or two in extent. There seems to be no recognised derivation of the curious name. At Shepherd's Bush, in 1657, one Miles Syndercomb hired a house for the purpose of assassinating Oliver Cromwell as he passed along the highroad to the town. The plot failed, and Syndercomb was hanged, drawn, and quartered in consequence. The precise spot on which the attempt took place is impossible to identify. It was somewhere near "the corner of Golders Lane," says Faulkner, but the lane has long since been obliterated.

St. Stephen's Church, in the Uxbridge Road, was the earliest church in this part of Hammersmith. It was built and endowed by Bishop Blomfield in 1850. Its tower and spire, rising to the height of 150 feet, can be seen for some distance.

St. Thomas's, in the Godolphin Road, is rather a pretty church of brick with red-tiled roof, and some ornamental stonework on the south face. It was built in 1882, designed by Sir A. Blomfield, and the foundation-stone was laid by the Baroness Burdett-Coutts. The chancel was added in 1887.

In Leysfield Road stands St. Andrew's Presbyterian Church, of which the foundation-stone was [Pg 29] laid by the present Duke of Argyll, March 30, 1870.

In the extreme west of the Goldhawk Road is St. Mary's Church, in bright red brick, erected 1886. The Duchess of Teck laid the foundation-stone. This has brought us to the end of the houses. Behind St. Mary's lie waste land and market-gardens. Just outside the parish boundary are two old houses of brick in the style of the seventeenth century; they used to be known as Stamford Brook Manor House, but they have no authentic history. Starch Green Road branches off from the Goldhawk Road opposite Ravenscourt Park; this road, running up into the Askew Road, was formerly known by the still more extraordinary name of Gaggle Goose Green.

In Cobbold Road, to the north of the waste land is St. Saviour's. An iron church was first erected here in 1884, and the present red-brick building was consecrated March 4, 1889. The chancel was only added in 1894.

In Becklow Road are a neat row of almshouses with gabled roofs. These are the Waste Land Almshouses. In the words of the charity report, ordered to be printed by the Vestry of Hammersmith in 1890, "This foundation owes its origin to a resolution which was entered into by the copyholders of the Manor on Fulham on the 23rd April, 1810, that no grants of waste land belong [Pg 30] ing to the manor should in future be applied to the purpose of raising a fund and endowing almshouses."

Part of the money received from the Waste Lands Fund thus created has been appropriated to the Fulham side, and part to the Hammersmith side. The Hammersmith almshouses were at first built at Starch Green. In 1868 these houses were pulled down and new ones erected. The present almshouses were erected in 1886 for twelve inmates.

In the Uxbridge Road, opposite Becklow Road, is St. Luke's Church, a red-brick building with no spire or tower, erected in 1872. The iron church which it succeeded, stands still behind it, and is used for a choir-room and vestry.

A short way westward, in the Uxbridge Road, is Oaklands Congregational Church, a somewhat heavy building covered with stucco, with a large portico supported by Corinthian columns.

Behind the houses bordering the north of the Uxbridge Road is a wide expanse of waste land with one or two farms. This part of the Manor of Fulham was leased in 1549 by Bishop Bonner to Edward, Duke of Somerset, under the name of the Manor of Wormholt Barns. Through the attainder of the Duke the Crown eventually obtained possession of it. It passed through various hands, and was split up at last into two [Pg 31] parts, Wormholt and Eynham lands; these two names are still preserved in Wormholt and Eynham Farms. In 1812 the Government took a lease of the northern part of the land for twenty-one years at an annual rent of £100, which was subsequently renewed. On part of this land was built the prison of Wormwood Scrubs in 1874. Part is used as a rifle-range, and to the north is a large public and military ground for exercising troops, etc. To the east of the prison are the Chandos and the North Kensington cricket and football ground.

The Prison walls enclose an area of sixteen acres. The building was all done by convict labour. To the south, without the walls, lie the houses of the officials, warders, etc. On the great towers by the gateway are medallions of John Howard and Elizabeth Fry. Within the courtyard are workshops, etc., and immediately opposite the gateway is a fine chapel with circular windows built of Portland stone. Four great "halls" stretch out northward, at right angles to the gates. These measure 387 feet in length, are four stories in height, and each provides accommodation for 360 prisoners. The three western ones are for men, that on the east for women. On the male side one "hall" is reserved for convicts doing their months of solitary confinement before passing on elsewhere. The men are employed as masons, carpenters, etc., the women in laundry and needle-work. The exercise- [Pg 32] grounds are large and airy; the situation is very healthy.

The next district, traversed by the Latymer Road, is a squalid, miserable quarter of the borough, with poor houses on either side. In Clifton Street is St. Gabriel's, the mission church of St. James's, a little brick building erected in 1883 by the parishioners and others.

Further northward, beyond the railway-bridge, is Holy Trinity Church. The foundation-stone was laid on Ascension Day, 1887, by the Duchess of Albany. It is a red-brick building with a fine east window decorated with stone tracery. Beyond this there is nothing further of interest except St. Mary's Roman Catholic cemetery at Kensal Green. It comprises thirty acres, and was opened in May, 1858. There are many notable names among those buried here, namely: Cardinals Wiseman and Manning; Clarkson Stanfield, R.A.; Dr. Rock, who was Curator of Ecclesiastical Antiquities in the South Kensington Museum; Adelaide A. Proctor, Panizzi, Prince Lucien Bonaparte, and others. To the west of the cemetery lies a network of interlacing railways, to the north a few streets, in one of which there is an iron church.

We have now made practical acquaintance with this vast borough, stretching from the river to Kensal Green, and including within its limits an [Pg 33] exceptional number of churches and chapels of all denominations. There are numerous convents, almshouses, and schools. Hammersmith has always been noted for its charities, and no bequest to its poor has ever been made without being doubled and trebled by subsequent gratuities. On a general survey, the three most interesting places within the boundaries seem to be: St. Paul's School, flourishing in Hammersmith, but not indigenous; Ravenscourt Park, with its aroma of old history, and the sternly practical institution of Wormwood Scrubs Prison. Hammersmith can boast not a few great names among its residents, by no means least that of the loyal Sir Nicholas Crispe; but with Kneller, Radcliffe, Worlidge, Morland, Thompson, Turner, and Morris, it has a goodly list.

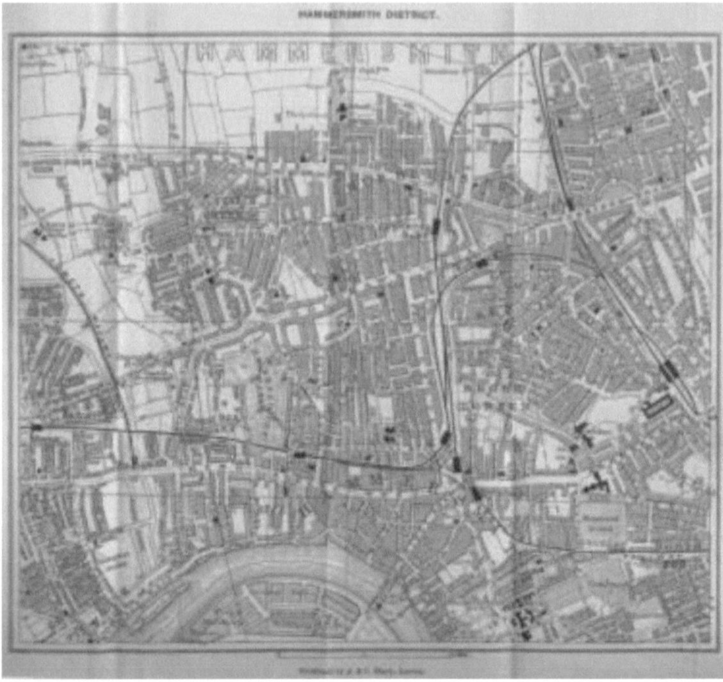

HAMMERSMITH DISTRICT.
Published by A. & C. Black, London.

[Pg 34]

FULHAM

The earliest authority for the derivation of the name of Fulham is Camden, in his "Britannia," who is quoted by all succeeding writers. Norden says: "Fulham, of the Saxons called Fullon-ham, which (as Master Camden taketh it) signifieth Volucrum Domus, the Habitacle of Birds or the Place of Fowls. Fullon and Furglas in the Saxon toong signifieth Fowles, and Ham or Hame as much as Home in our Toong. So that Fullonham or Fuglahame is as much as to say the Home House or Habitacle of Fowle. Ham also in many places signifieth Amnis a River. But it is most probable it should be of Land Fowle which usually haunt Groves and Clusters of Trees whereof in this Place it seemeth to have been plenty."

Bowack also quotes Camden, adding: "In all Probability a Place where all sorts of Water Fowls were bred and preserved for the Diversion of our Saxon Monarchs."

Lysons, commenting on this derivation, adds in [Pg 35] a note: "The Saxon word *ful* is translated foul: *fuhl*, a fowl: *full* and *fullan* are full, as *full mona*, the full moon." This latter meaning has been chosen by the authors of the Anglo-Saxon dictionaries, notably Somner, Lye, and Bosworth.

Fulham is bounded by Chelsea and Kensington on the east, by the river on the west and south, and by Hammersmith on the north. The eastern boundary follows generally the railway-line between Addison Road Station and the river, and the northern one is identical with the southern one of Hammersmith already given. The earliest record we have of Fulham is in 691, when a grant of the manor was made by Tyrtilus, Bishop of Hereford, to Erkenwald, Bishop of London, and his successors. In 879 a body of Danes made Fulham their winter quarters, and amused themselves by constructing the moat around the palace. Norden tells us that Henry III. often "lay" at the palace, and on two occasions Bishop Bancroft received visits here from Queen Elizabeth. James I. also came here before his coronation. In 1627 Charles I. dined with Bishop Montaigne. In 1642 the Parliamentary army encamped at Fulham, 24,000 strong, under Essex.

If we enter the borough of Fulham at the Hammersmith end, we come upon one of the most interesting associations of the whole district, just before the North End Road makes a decided bend. [Pg 36] Here are two houses, formerly one, called the Grange, in which the novelist Samuel Richardson passed the greater part of his life. This pompous, vain little man, who never to the end of his life abated one whit of his savage envy of his successful contemporaries, was endowed with the genius of originality which prompted him to write as no one had ever thought of writing before. He remained here until 1755, when he moved to Parsons Green. He had begun life as one of the nine children of a man of small means, and was apprenticed to a printer. This work he carried on long after the necessity for it had ceased, for he was above all things punctual, methodical, neat, and entirely the opposite in character to that usually ascribed to genius. To a man of his type it seems almost sinful to give up routine work in order to depend on the work of imagination. He had a house at Salisbury Court near his business premises, and the Grange at North End was his country residence. Here he composed "Sir Charles Grandison" and "Clarissa," writing for the most part in a grotto in the garden, where the admiring circle of women who adored him, and whose effusive flattery he ever received with pleasure, paid court to him. He was twice married, and while at North End was living with his second wife and their four daughters. Thus he was surrounded by womenkind, who forgave [Pg 37] him all faults on account of his appreciation of sentimentality.

The house is distinctly picturesque. The southern half is of red brick, and is surrounded by a high wall, in which is a gateway with tall red-brick piers surmounted by stone balls. Over the wall hangs an acacia-tree, and on the front of the house is an old sundial—altogether a house one could well associate with an imaginative novelist. It was the residence of the late Sir Edward Burne-Jones, Bart. The other part of the house has been painted a light stone colour. Even as early as 1813 the Grange had been divided into two houses.

St. Mary's Church, facing the Hammersmith Road, is in Fulham. It was built by a Mr. Richard Hunt, to whose memory there is a tablet on the wall, and was opened as a chapel of ease in 1814. Some fine carving on the north side of the chancel and the oak panelling of the gallery were brought from Lady Mary Coke's old mansion at Chiswick.

In 1860 the site of Edith Road was, according to Crofton Croker, to be let on building lease. In it, Croker says, "once stood the house of Cipriani." But there is some doubt as to the exact site of Cipriani's house, which is also claimed for Great Church Lane, Hammersmith (see p. 7). Cipriani lived in England from 1755 to 1785, and his works [Pg 38] were largely engraved by Bartolozzi, who also had a house at North End.

Further south, to the east of Queen's Club grounds, are a maze of new streets, in one of which, Castletown Road, is a large and fine Congregational chapel and hall. The chapel has a square tower rising to a considerable height, and the roof is supported by flying buttresses. This is an offshoot of the Allen Street Congregational Chapel, whose trustees still have the control and help to support it financially. The foundation-stone was the last laid by the late Earl of Shaftesbury, November 22, 1882.

The well-known Earl's Court Exhibition has an entrance in the North End Road. It occupies the area between this on the one side, and Eardley Crescent and Philbeach Gardens on the other, and is the largest exhibition open in London. It belongs partly to Kensington and partly to Fulham, for the boundary line is close to the railway.

St. Andrew's Church, at the corner of Greyhound and Vereker Roads, was built in 1873. It has a spire, and differs little from the accepted model.

The entrance to Queen's Club grounds is in the Comeragh Road. On the right of the gate is a grand-stand, from which a fine view of the eleven or twelve acres of ground can be obtained. Along the west side run the principal buildings, including [Pg 39] secretary's offices, grand-stands, tennis and fives courts, etc. The covered lawn-tennis courts are laid with great care and expense, the floors being of American maple, screwed and fitted over a patent wooden floor to insure absolute accuracy. The ladies' lawn-tennis championship is played off here. The great public event of the year is the Oxford and Cambridge sports, which in interest rank after the boat-race and cricket-match.

Close to Queen's Club is the Hammersmith cemetery, an extensive piece of ground of some twenty acres. There is a broad gravel walk down the centre, and two small chapels, round which the graves are thickly clustered, spreading gradually westward as space is required. The first burial took place in 1869. The principal entrance is in the Margravine Road. The significance of this unexpected name in such a position is explained by the fact that the Margravine of Brandenburg-Anspach had a house near the river in this part for many years. It is described in detail below.

Just across the road is the Fulham and Hammersmith Union Workhouse and Infirmary, facing Fulham Palace Road. Between the workhouse and the river is a stretch of land used by market-gardeners. It was by the riverside that Brandenburg House, built by Sir Nicholas Crispe in the beginning of Charles I.'s reign, was situated. [Pg 40] General Fairfax quartered himself here in 1647 during the Civil War, and his troops afterwards plundered the house; but at the close of the war Sir Nicholas returned and restored his property to its former state. After his death in 1666 it descended to his nephew, who sold it seventeen years later to Prince Rupert, who gave it to Margaret Hughes. It passed through the possession of various owners. One of these, George Dodington, afterwards Lord Melcombe, repaired and modernized it, altering the name to La Trappe. In 1792 it became the property of the Margrave of Brandenburg-Anspach and Bayreuth, and at his death the Margravine, formerly Lady Craven, continued to live there. Faulkner gives a minute account of the house and a long inventory of all the pictures in it while it was the residence of this lady. She built a theatre near the waterside, and herself took part in the performances. Bills of the plays in which her name appears are still extant. One of them is preserved in the Hammersmith Free Library. Though Brandenburg House was situated in Fulham, it is often described and spoken of as in Hammersmith. This is perhaps owing to its connection with Sir Nicholas Crispe, who was a great benefactor to the latter parish, and perhaps because the house existed when Hammersmith and Fulham were still one parish. Lysons says that during the [Pg 41] interregnum it was proposed to make the hamlet of Hammersmith parochial, and add to it Sir Nicholas Crispe's house and a part of North End, but, as stated, the separation of the parishes did not take place until 1834.

On May 3, 1820, Queen Caroline, wife of George IV., came to live at Brandenburg House, and on the fifteenth of that month was presented with a congratulatory address by the inhabitants of Hammersmith. On the abandonment of the Bill of "Pains and Penalties" by the House of Lords she received a second address. She had been petitioned by people of all classes and conditions during the progress of the Bill, the demonstration of the watermen and lightermen of the Thames on October 8 having been especially noticeable. The Queen had stood on the balcony of her residence and bowed her acknowledgments to the enthusiastic crowd. The Queen died in 1821, and the King caused the house to be destroyed shortly afterwards, it is said, in jealousy of her popularity.

In a villa near Brandenburg House lived Mrs. Billington, the famous singer, who died at Venice in 1818. At her death Sir John Sibbald, a Civil Servant of the East India Company, and at one time Ambassador to the Court of Hyder Ali Khan, bought the house. It was tenanted later by the novelist Captain Marryat, R.N. South [Pg 42] ward there is a large extent of ground devoted to market-gardens, for which Fulham has long been famous. This is broken only by a few houses about Crabtree Alley and Crabtree Lane. Close to the latter is St. Clement's Church, of yellow brick, consecrated in 1886. The reredos painting is in the early Florentine style, and represents the Resurrection. There are several stained-glass windows and a handsome wrought-iron chancel-screen. The font and its cover were originally at St. Matthew's, Friday Street. Opposite to the church is a public recreation-ground, and south of it the Fulham cemetery, not so large, but more thickly planted with shrubs than that of Hammersmith, already noted.

St. James's Diocesan Home for Penitents is on the river side of the Fulham Palace Road. It was originally established in 1856, though it was not then in Hammersmith. Funds failed, and the institution would have come to an untimely end but for the intervention of the then Bishop of London, who made the Home diocesan; the present building was erected in 1871. The total number of inmates at present is 76. These are employed at laundry and needle work, etc. The penitents are divided into three classes, and are employed according to their position. Very nearly opposite to the Home are the Fulham Waste Land and Lygon Almshouses. The buildings form two [Pg 43] sides of a square, the sides being respectively for married and single pensioners. The latter may be of either sex. The married couples have two rooms and a small scullery, and receive 8s. a week. The single persons have one room, with 5s. per week. The houses are neatly built of brick with slate roofs and high chimneys. In the centre there is a room used as a chapel. There are altogether fourteen inmates. On a stone let into the wall nearest the road is the inscription: "The Fulham Waste Land and Lygon Almshouses, founded 1833 and rebuilt 1886. This stone was laid by Frederick, Lord Bishop of London, April 21, 1886."

The origin of the double name was in this wise: The vestry of the parish of Fulham and Hammersmith in 1810 had a fund of money derived from the enclosure of certain waste lands belonging to the parish. By 1833 this fund had so much increased that it was resolved to build almshousess, which were accordingly erected on a piece of land in the Dawes Road. In the beginning of the eighties Lady Lygon bought a piece of land in the Fulham Palace Road for the purpose of founding almshouses on it. This project was never carried out, and the ground was eventually given to the Waste Land Trustees, who built the present almshouses on it in 1886.

The part of Fulham to the east of the Fulham [Pg 44] Palace Road is very dreary; long, dull streets, lined by small houses and varied by small chapels and big Board schools, constitute an area at the best highly respectable, and at the worst squalid. It is useless to enumerate all the churches and chapels that have sprung up here, particularly as there are none of any architectural or historical interest. They have been built from time to time to meet the rapid increase of population in a growing district that will doubtless soon spread over the market-gardens that now reach the river. The principal churches are St. Augustine's, in Lillie Road, of red brick with freestone dressings; and St. Peter's, in Reporton Road, which contains a pulpit that might make more ancient churches proud, for it is of carved oak, and is supposed to be the work of Grinling Gibbons. It came from St. Matthew's, Friday Street. The Church of St. Thomas of Canterbury in Rylston Road is Roman Catholic, and was designed by Pugin, who also designed the altars and reredos of the minor chapels in it.

Lillie Road is so named after Sir John Lillie, who was a director of the East India Company and lived at Fulham. To Normand House in Normand Road there is some interest attached. The name is supposed to be a corruption of "No-man." Bowack alludes to it thus: "There is also a handsome ancient seat in Fulham Field called [Pg 45] No-Man's-Land House, now belonging to —— Wild, Esq. The piece of ground which it stands on was known as No-Man's-Land." The date 1664 is worked into the iron scroll-work of a gateway. The house has been considerably added to from time to time, but the wide, low passage with its pretty archways and panelling, which is seen on entrance, is distinctly one of the oldest parts. Two staircases, one of which is carved with the Tudor roses, are very picturesque. Many of the rooms are panelled. Crofton Croker gives the date incorrectly as 1661. He adds: "It is said to have been used as a hospital for persons recovering from the Great Plague in 1665." Sir E. Bulwer Lytton resided here at one time. Later on it was used as a lunatic asylum, and was so when Thorne wrote his "Environs" in 1876. It is now the Community of the Sisters of St. Katherine for the work of assisting and rescuing young women convicted of a first offence or discharged for dishonesty without conviction, but otherwise of good moral character. The girls are employed in house and laundry work, which is taken in from outside, and the proceeds go to the funds. After two years' training they are placed in service. This institution has a branch at Hammersmith, and a small one at Walham. It belongs to the Church of England. In Lillie Road, to the east of North End Road, is the Mount Carmel [Pg 46] Hermitage. This convent is a red-brick building with a small chapel attached, erected in 1880 by some French Sisters who had come to London in 1865, and settled at Fulham in 1867 in a house near the site of the present convent. There are eleven nuns, of whom three are lay Sisters. They are devoted to the contemplative life. Just opposite is a large brewery, established 1867. At the east end of Eustace Road is a small brick Wesleyan chapel, hidden away in a corner, which deserves a word of mention, as it is a German chapel and the services are in that language.

The Fulham Congregational Church in Dawes Road is a large building of red brick with stone facings, opened on April 5, 1887. There is a lecture-room beneath, besides library, class-rooms, and infant Sunday-school.

We have now arrived at Walham Green, once a small village standing in the fields. It has been variously spelt. In a map of 1686 by Lea it is "Wollam," and in 1706 "Wallam"; in a 1720 map (Seale) it is "Wallom," and in Rocque of 1754 "Wallam" again. Before 1686 it was Wandon and Wansdon, according to Crofton Croker, and Lysons derives it from Wendon, either because the traveller had to wend his way through it to Fulham, or because the drainage from higher grounds "wandered" through it to the river. The Church of St. John is situated at Walham [Pg 47] Green. It has a high square tower with corner pinnacles, and is partly covered with ivy. It is built of stone, and the total cost was about £9,680. It was consecrated on August 14, 1828, and restored in 1892-93. The schools in connection with it, built in 1894, stand in the Dawes Road opposite. Passing eastward on the Fulham Road, we come to the Walham Green Station of the District Railway. Just opposite is the Town Hall, a square building of brick with stone frontage, ornamentally decorated with carving. It was built in 1891. Further on, on the opposite side, is the Wesleyan Chapel at Walham Green, opened in April, 1892. The buildings are of brick, with stone dressings. In the Moore Park Road, which branches off the Fulham Road near the boundary, stands St. James's Church, an ugly brick building with no spire or tower, which was consecrated on June 28, 1867, and the apse was built out at the east end about a dozen years later. There is a row of stained-glass windows low down across the west end. Going back to Walham Green proper, we find a double row of almshouses, shut off from the Vanston Place Road by iron gates. These are the almshouses of the Butchers' Charitable Institution, which was founded on October 16, 1828. The almshouses themselves were begun at Walham Green in 1840. The object is described in the report as "for affording relief to decayed or [Pg 48] distressed master butchers, master pork-butchers, cattle and meat commission salesmen, their widows and orphans."

In Fulham Road, westward, John Rocque lived. His maps of London and environs are still used by all topographers, and are full of accurate detail. In the map published in 1741-45 his name is printed across the road at this spot. On the south side of the road formerly stood Ravensworth House, pulled down in 1877. The site of it is now occupied by the Swan Brewery. The grounds of Ravensworth House stretched out as far as the present railway, where there was a large pond. When Thorne wrote his "Environs" in 1876, the house was still standing, and he describes it as of "but moderate proportions, but more capacious than it looks." The Queen and Prince Consort were entertained here by Lord Ravensworth in 1840. Faulkner refers to Ravensworth House as "Mr. Ord's house and garden," and mentions the Glastonbury thorn which flowered on Christmas Day, and the moss-rose which, being "laid" year after year, at length covered a space in diameter 47 feet. The Swan Brewery, owned by Messrs. Stansfeld, was founded on the same site in 1765. It passed through several hands, and eventually, in 1880, Messrs. Stansfeld acquired possession and proceeded to erect new premises. Bolingbroke House was a little further on. Tradition says it [Pg 49] was the residence of Lord Bolingbroke, who was visited here by Pope. It was eventually divided into two houses—Dungannon House and Albany Lodge—and these were demolished only in 1893. Dungannon House was also known as Acacia Cottage, and in it lived the first publisher of Cowper's works—a Mr. Joseph Johnson—until 1809.

We are now at Purser's Cross, and after a digression southward shall presently return. East End House, pulled down in 1885, stood at the corner where Delvino Road now joins the Green. It was the residence for some time of Mrs. Fitzherbert, morganatic wife of George, Prince of Wales, afterwards George IV. It was built by Sir Francis Child, Lord Mayor of London in 1699, and was a plain white house. Admiral Sir Charles Wager and Dr. Ekins, Dean of Carlisle, lived here at different times. The gardens stretched over much of the land now built upon at the back, and contained a magnificent cedar-tree, which had to be blown up by dynamite when the house was pulled down. Sir Thomas Bodley, founder of the Bodleian Library at Oxford, lived at Parson's Green from 1605 to 1609 (Lysons).

At the back of a network of small streets to the east lies Eelbrook Common. In Faulkner's map, 1813, it is marked Hell-brook, though in the printed matter he uses both titles. It has [Pg 50] been suggested that the title may have originally been Hill-brook, as there was a curious rise in the ground just to the west; but, on the other hand, eels may have been common in the pond above referred to. Faulkner gives a notice relative to it embodied in an order relating to Wormholt Wood, presented at a court held for the Manor of Fulham on May 9, 1603, which runs as follows: "That no person or persons shall put in any horse or other cattle into Hell-brook until the last day of April every year henceforth: nor shall not at any time after the 11th of May put in nor take out any of their said cattles, any other way but the old and accustomed way upon pain to forfeit to the lord for every such offence £01.00.00." In 1656 Colonel Edmund Harvey, who had bought the manor confiscated under the Commonwealth, agreed to pay fifty shillings yearly to the poor for taking in the common called Hell-brook. Through part of the land included in Eelbrook Common runs the District Railway between Walham Green and Parsons Green stations.

We now return to the junction of Parson's Green Lane and Fulham Road, called Purser's Cross, which has been variously written Persicross, Percycross. The stone bearing inscription "Purser's Cross, 7th of August 1738," is built into the wall of the corner house, now a grocer's shop. It was originally in the house on the same site occupied [Pg 51] for a time by Madame Grisi. The stone itself is very small, about 8 by 6 inches, and, being high up, is rather difficult to see. The story goes that the place was so called in memory of a highwayman, who, being overtaken at the cross-roads, shot himself after flinging his purse into the crowd, and was buried here with a stake driven through his body. Purser's Cross is mentioned in the parish books in 1602.

Arundel Gardens were built over the site of Arundel House, demolished in 1898.

The origin of the name Arundel House is not known. It seems probable that the house was originally a Tudor structure, as some unmistakable Tudor mullions were found built up in an old wall; yet the greater part of it dated from the Stuart period. A large ornamental cistern which stood in the scullery bore date 1703. The back view of the house, with its irregular dark-brick buildings and additions, here and there covered with creepers, was very picturesque. Tradition says that Henry Hallam, the historian, lived here about 1819.

Close at hand stands the Fulham Free Public Library. It came into existence in 1886, when an old building, standing a few feet back from the main Fulham Road, was adapted for offices, lending and reference rooms, and a new reading-room of magnificent dimensions—70 by 30 [Pg 52] feet, and 22 feet in height—was added at a cost of £6,000. This was opened by the then Bishop of London, October 20, 1888.

Further westward, at the entrance of Chesilton Place, stands Munster Park Wesleyan Chapel, with a square tower surmounted by four high pinnacles. It was opened in 1882.

At the west entrance of the Munster Road stood Munster House, demolished in 1895. Faulkner spells it Mustow or Munster, and in John Rocque's Survey of 1741-45 it is "Muster." Lysons says: "Mustow (commonly called Munster) House on the north side of the road to London between Fulham and Purses Cross was during the greater part of the last century the property of the Powells, from whom it came to Sir John Williams of Pengethly, Monmouthshire, Baronet. It is now the property of Arthur Annesley Powell, Esq., and is occupied as a school." Faulkner mentions the tradition of its having been a hunting-seat of King Charles II. Croker says it is supposed to owe its name to Melesina Schulenberg, created by George II. Duchess of Munster. For some time before it was pulled down it was used as a lunatic asylum.

From Munster Road onwards the houses on the south side of the Fulham Road are not aggressively new. In the grounds of one of them—Eridge House—there is a fine cedar, which shows [Pg 53] that the grounds must have belonged to some building older than that standing at present, probably that of Fulham Lodge. On the east of the High Street stand All Saints' National Schools. In the continuation of the High Street is an old house on the left-hand side called Fulham House. It stands back on the east side of the road behind a wall. Some of the carving on the fireplaces and doors is very elaborate. In a large room upstairs a sumptuously carved wooden mantel encloses a coloured marble block with a white marble centre. The door of this room is also very fine. The cellars are extraordinarily large and massively built. This used to be called Stourton House. Faulkner mentions that in 1449 John Sherbourn and others sold a house and garden at Fulham, then valued at 3s. 4d. per annum, to John, first Lord Stourton, and it remained in possession of the family many years. The Fulham Pottery and Cheavin Filter Company stands just at the corner of the New King's Road and Burlington Street. The business was established here by John Dwight in 1671. Specimens of his stone-ware are to be seen in the British Museum, which in 1887 acquired twelve new examples. It is said that John Dwight, M.A., of Christ Church College, Oxford, was the inventor of porcelain in England. He also discovered the mystery of the Cologne ware, and successfully competed with it [Pg 54] in England. Doulton himself, the founder of the great Doulton ware, was an apprentice at Fulham. In 1840 the buildings were greatly enlarged and improved, and again in 1864. The ornamental pottery which is still made—though in a small quantity—resembles Doulton ware, but the great development of the industry has been in the direction of glazed ware of great resisting power. Cheavin's patent filters are sent all over the world, and a speciality is made of the chemical trade, immense baths for the electro-plating acids being supplied to Government.

Close at hand, at the back of High Street, stood the old workhouse, which has been for many years pulled down. At the back of the High Street also was a gaol for female convicts, which has now vanished. The gaol was built about 1854 on the site of Burlington House, which had been a school.

Church Row is a charming old-fashioned row, and the houses mentioned by Bowack as "very handsome and airy" are probably those still standing. At the end of the row are Sir William Powell's Almshouses, prettily designed with red-tiled roofs, and at one end is a tower surmounted by statues of female characters from the Bible. Directly across the road is the old rectory-house. A shady avenue of young limes leads up to the church. The tower, which is square, is shown in [Pg 55] old prints to have been surmounted by a steeple. It contains a peal of bells cast by Ruddle in the middle of the eighteenth century; all the bells bear inscriptions, and many of them the date of casting. Within the church porch is a board with the following words: "1881. The Parish Church of All Saints, Fulham, lapsed into a state of decay, and, being subject to the floods from the river Thames, was pulled down and rebuilt. In the construction of the present church, stones belonging to three previous churches, the oldest of which apparently dated from the twelfth century, were discovered.

"The east end has been carried nine feet, and the south wall five feet, beyond the limits of the previous church, while the floor of the nave has been raised two feet nine inches, and the roof thirteen feet above the former levels. The cornerstone at the east angle of the north transept was laid by Archibald Campbell Tait, 1880, and the church was re-consecrated by John Jackson, Bishop of London, on July 9th, 1881."

The monuments preserved from the older buildings stand in the church in rather different order from formerly. In the west end is that in remembrance of Viscount Mordaunt, son of the Earl of Peterborough. It is a statue of a man larger than life; the figure, which is carved in marble, has a proud and defiant attitude. It stands on a slab of [Pg 56] black marble supported by a pedestal. On either side on smaller pedestals are the Viscount's coronet and gauntlets. He is in Roman dress, and holds a baton as Constable of Windsor Castle. On the left is his pedigree engraved on marble. The date inscribed on the tablet to his memory is 1675. At the west end of the north aisle is the ancient font mentioned by Faulkner as standing in the east end of the south aisle. It was the gift of Mr. Thomas Hyll, churchwarden in 1622, and is of stone, painted and gilt. On the east wall of the north aisle are three monuments which attract attention. That of "Payne of Pallenswick Esqre," who "hath placed this monument to the memory of himself and Jane his wife who hath lived with him in wedlock XLIIII years and died the first day of May in Anno Dmi 1610, and the said William Payne the day of ____ Anno Dmi ____. The sayd William Payne hath given forever after his decease an Ilande in the Ryver of Thames caled Makenshawe to the use of the poor of this parish on Hammersmith side." The date of his own death not having been filled in, it is probable he is buried elsewhere. Next to his is the monument of Thomas Bonde, dated March, 1600, with a quaint inscription beginning: "At Earth in Cornwell was my first begininge, from Bondes and Corringtons as it may apere." Next to this is the monument of Katharine Hart, of [Pg 57] which a representation is given by Faulkner. She is kneeling with her two sons and two daughters, in a style similar to the Lawrence monument in Chelsea Old Church. The inscription bears date 1605. On the north side of the chancel is a large monument to Sir Thomas Smith, died November 28, 1609. Opposite is that of Lady Margaret Legh, who is represented life-size dressed in stiff ruff and farthingale, holding an infant in swaddling bands on her knee. Another infant in swaddling bands is on her left side. Over her is an arch supported by pillars. The coat of arms of her family rests in the centre of the arch. She died July 3, 1603. The monument has been very much admired. In the southern aisle is the organ, with handsomely carved oak case. On a jutting wall close by is a curious old brass plate found buried in 1770. The inscription is in Latin to Margaret Svanders, who died 1529. The floor of the church is thickly covered with flat tombstones. One of these is in memory of Thomas Carlos, son of Colonel Careless, who hid in the oak-tree with King Charles II., and who was consequently allowed to change his name to Carlos, and to bear upon his arms a branching oak-tree. The coat of arms on the tomb is very distinct, and the date 1665.

Opposite to the Peterborough monument at the west end is a very large marble monument in memory of Dorothy Clarke, and her second [Pg 58] husband. A great marble urn upon it is said by Bowack to have been the work of Grinling Gibbons, and to have cost £300. A memorial window to Archbishop Tait is fixed in the west end of the south aisle. In the churchyard are the tombs of Bishops Compton, Robinson, Gibson, Sherlock, Hayter, Terrick, and Lowth. Here also is the grave of Theodore Hook, the wit, with a perfectly plain stone at the head recording his death, "24th Aug. 1841 in the 53rd year of his age."

Near the entrance to what are now the public gardens stood Pryor's Bank, a well-known house, built about the beginning of the eighteenth century in an ancient style. It was originally called Vine Cottage, and was very elaborately fitted up. Nearly all the doors were surrounded with carving and golding. Many of them were of solid oak, and the panelling in the rooms corresponded. Two quaint old panels of painted wood in one of the reception-rooms bore curious figures on pedestals; underneath one who was in ecclesiastical robes was written: "John Baylis, Lord Pryor, 1554, of Werlock Abbey"; and under the other: "William of Wickham, 1366, Bishop of Winchester." Close by Pryor's Bank stood Egmont Lodge, where Theodore Hook lived. It was a small house, pulled down in 1855. The aspect of the whole of this part has been completely changed [Pg 59] of late years by the building of a river-wall, and the laying out as a public garden of the strip of ground by the river called Bishop's Park.

The grounds of this public park are decorated with flower-beds and supplied with seats. On part of the space once stood Craven Cottage, built by the Margravine of Brandenburg when she was Countess Craven. Sir E. Bulwer-Lytton lived here from 1840 to 1846. At the beginning of Bishop's Avenue is the entrance to the Manor House, or Fulham Palace, as it is commonly called, the residence of the Bishop of London. Passing between two lodges of red brick, and following a short drive, we come to a massive gateway with heavy oak doors. Through this lies the first courtyard, very little altered from Faulkner's print in 1813. The Manor of Fulham, as we have seen already, has belonged to the See of London since about 691, when it was given to Bishop Erkenwald and his successors by "Tyrtilus, a bishop, with the consent of Sigehard, king of the east Saxons and the king of the Mercians." Lysons adds that Tyrtilus, Bishop of Hereford, who he supposes is intended, was contemporary with Erkenwald. In 1647 it was sold to Colonel Harvey with the leasehold land belonging to it for £7,617 8s. 10d., but was given back to the See at the Restoration. In Domesday Book we read: "In Fulham the Bishop of London holds forty [Pg 60] hides.... Its whole value is forty pounds, the like when received in Edward's [the Confessor's] time fifty pounds."

The carriage-entrance is in Fulham Palace Road, and this leads to an avenue of limes. To the north lies a part of the public park, once a field belonging to the Bishops. The drive crosses the wonderful moat, which is nearly a mile in circuit, and, if dug by the Danes as conjectured, must be a thousand years old. This moat has given rise to much discussion, as it is too far from the palace for any purpose of defence, and the idea that it was made by the Danes as a partial safeguard against the floods of the river is that which gains most credence.

The palace is built round two courtyards, and the one first entered is by far the older. It was built by Bishop Fitzjames in the reign of Henry VII., and the great gateway which leads to it bears his arms cut in stone. There are few places that preserve so completely their ancient aspect as this courtyard; the material is red brick, and in summer, when creepers climb over the worn bricks, its attractiveness is greatly enhanced. The wing on the west or river side contains the rooms used by Laud while Bishop; this part has been refaced, and the buttresses were added at the same time, but within it is unchanged. Opposite, on the eastern side, are the rooms once occu [Pg 61] pied by Bishop Bonner, which carry an association no less interesting, though of a different kind. The great porch facing the entrance gateway leads into the hall, which is also part of Bishop Fitzjames's work. The hall is divided by a screen of dark oak, which came from old Doctors' Commons, and the other oak fittings were brought here from the former chapel, and originally belonged to the chapel of London House, Aldersgate Street. A new ceiling was put up by Bishop Sherlock, whose arms are over the fireplace, in conjunction with a framed inscription recording the building of Bishop Fitzjames on a site where buildings had stood as far back as the Conquest. The hall was at one time used as the chapel, of which more will be told presently. In the same block is the kitchen, once the dining-room.

In 1715 Bishop Robinson presented a petition to the Archbishop of Canterbury, stating that the palace was in a ruinous condition, and was too large for the revenues. A number of commissioners, amongst whom were Sir John Vanbrugh and Sir Christopher Wren, were accordingly appointed to examine into the matter and report upon it. The purport of their report was that, after taking down "the bakehouse and the pastry-house, which adjoined to the kitchen, and all the buildings to the northward of the great dining-room, there would be left between fifty and sixty [Pg 62] rooms beside the chapel, hall, and kitchen." These being judged sufficient for the use of the Bishop, a license was granted to pull down what was superfluous and put the rest into better condition.

However, in 1764 Bishop Terrick began a further extension and rebuilding, and it is to him we owe the idea of the second quadrangle or courtyard. He died too soon to complete his project, and left only the western wing of the new courtyard, but his work was carried on by his successor, Sherlock. The design was distinctly good, particularly for that age of debased taste. Engravings of Sherlock's palace show battlemented angle towers, and a recessed main building which is very picturesque. In the southern wing he placed the library and dining-room, and on the eastern side he made the chapel. When Bishop Howley came into power, he set to work at once to alter the palace of his predecessors, and replace it by something which can only be described as a block. He levelled the frontage between the towers, and cut off the battlements, and made the building much as we see it now, with the exception of the modernization of some of the windows. Howley then converted the building made for the chapel into the library, which it still remains. It includes the famous collection of books made by Bishop Porteous. [Pg 63] The rooms on the south side became under Bishop Howley's modifications the dining and drawing rooms, and the great hall he used for a chapel.

It was not until 1867, under Bishop Tait, that the present chapel was opened. It is connected with the main building by a passage, and stands on the river side of the palace. It was designed by Mr. Butterfield, and is bright and well proportioned. Behind the altar at present stands a reredos of carved wood with a representation of the Crucifixion.

The palace grounds have been considerably curtailed by the formation of the public park, which now bounds them riverwards. The idea of giving this portion of land to the public was carried out by Bishop Temple, though it originated with his predecessor. The park includes the long strip above mentioned, lying outside the moat, and the field to the north already spoken of in connection with the drive. The embankment has entirely altered the aspect of this part of Fulham, and the days when the Bishop of London "took water" at his private stairs have gone for ever.

Within the palace gardens are many curious specimens of trees not found elsewhere in England. Bishop Grindal was the first of the Bishops to take an interest in gardening, but it is to Bishop [Pg 64] Compton that we owe the real beauty of the gardens. He was bold enough to defy James II., and to declare in the House of Lords that the civil and ecclesiastical constitution of the kingdom was in danger; he further incensed the King by refusing to suspend a clergyman who had preached a sermon against Roman Catholicism. For this he himself was suspended, and not allowed to exercise his ecclesiastical functions, though, as according to the law, the temporalities of the see were his own—they could not be touched. The Bishop therefore retired to Fulham and sought solace among his plants, to the great gain of his successors in the See.

But the palace and its grounds have occupied us long enough, and the ramble through Fulham must be resumed.

A small footbridge leads across the moat to the churchyard. Crossing this, we find ourselves in Church Row, which brings us to the junction of the New King's Road and the old High Street. Following the New King's Road and passing under the railway, we come almost immediately to the shady drive leading to Mulgrave House. Adjoining the grounds of Mulgrave House are those of Hurlingham Club, which cover fifty acres, and include a picturesque lake. Pigeon-shooting, polo-playing, tennis, and archery are all provided for. The entrance in the Hurlingham [Pg 65] Road leads to a well-kept drive, which takes us straight up to the club-house. The house is of white stone, and the front facing the river has an arcade supported by enormous pillars running right up to the cornice. On the west side is a fine conservatory, on the east the large dining-rooms and smoking-lounge, which have been added to meet requirements. Within the house itself the drawing-room and coffee-room have been ornamented with coloured designs on ceiling and walls, and are very bright and handsomely furnished. Many of the rooms upstairs have ornamented carved cornices and panels. The club was started in 1867, mainly for pigeon-shooting, under the auspices of Mr. Frank Heathcote, who leased it from Mr. Naylor. Before that time the house had been the residence of the Horsley-Palmers and of Lord Egremont. In 1874 the property was bought by the club, and polo-playing was begun. The King and Queen—as Prince and Princess of Wales—and Duke and Duchess of Edinburgh watched the first game in the June of that year.

The ancient history of the house is defective. In the churchwarden's accounts of the parish in 1681 we read: "It is ordered that there be built and erected two small tenements next to the north side of ye poore Almes Houses given by John Lappy with such old stuff as was lately [Pg 66] taken downe from the Pest Houses in Hurlingham Field at ye charge of the Parish contayning two roomes." And Faulkner adds an extract from Brayley's "London" to the above in the form of a note: "Hurlingham Field is now the property of the Earl of Ranelagh, and the site of his house. It was here that great numbers of people were buried during the plague." The origin of the name seems lost in obscurity, though it has been suggested, perhaps facetiously, it was derived from the custom of hurling the bodies of the plague dead into any grave without care or compunction. Broom House, next door, with adjoining grounds, is noticed in Rocque's 1757 map, and is inscribed on Faulkner's 1813 map as "Broom Houses." Faulkner refers to it as a little village, but mentions that "the Dowager Countess of Lonsdale has an elegant house and garden here in full view of the Thames." The place is said to have received its name from the broom which grew here profusely. Broomhouse Road runs from Hurlingham Road, past the gates of Broom House, down to the river. It is a veritable lane, with leafy trees shadowing it. On the east side, a little above Broom House, is a very striking building of red brick, with bright white stone facings, and a square central tower surmounted by four pinnacles. This is the Elizabeth Free School, founded and endowed by [Pg 67] Mr. Sulivan of Broom House, in 1855. Further down the road, close by the river, is Carnwath House, the residence of the Earl of Carnwath. It is irregularly built of brick. Beyond it is a raised path, which winds along by the river and leads past acres of market-gardens, in which are large plum-orchards.

Northward is Parsons Green, so called from the fact that the old rectory-house stood on the west side. Lysons says: "Parsonage house stands upon the west side of Parsons or Parsonage Green, to which it gave its name. It is now divided into two tenements. In the year 1598 it was in the tenure of Sir Francis Walsingham's widow." Bowack, in 1705, wrote that it was old and much decayed. He says an old stone building adjoining seemed to be 300 or 400 years old, and might have been used for religious services by the Rectors and their households. Parson's Green was once a very fashionable place; in Strype's edition of Stow's "Survey" it is commented on as having "very good houses for gentry." St. Dionis' Church is a noticeable object, built of red brick, with Bath stone dressings. Though only consecrated on June 18, 1885, it carries with it associations from an older building, St. Dionis Backchurch, which stood at the corner of Lime Street and Fenchurch Street. When that church had been pulled down, the pulpit, font, and altar were [Pg 68] transferred to the new building at Fulham, and £10,000 was devoted out of the proceeds of the sale of the site for the use and endowment of the new church. The pulpit and font date from 1666. The plate also is interesting, including two flagons, four chalices, four patens, etc., which are of various dates from 1625 to 1725. A large red-brick hall, separated from the church by Rectory Road, is used as a mission-hall. A few steps further northward, partly hidden from the road by intervening buildings, was the old house called Rosamund's Bower. Before its demolition in 1892 it was quaintly pretty, with leaded window-panes and red-tiled roof, and was then known as Audley Cottage. It was called Rosamond's Bower first in order to perpetuate the tradition of its standing on the site of a mansion of Fair Rosamund. The earliest mention of it is in 1480, when it was valued at ten marks per annum. It belonged to Sir Michael Wharton before 1725, and when he died in that year it was divided between his co-heirs. It was the residence of Mr. Crofton Croker between 1837 and 1846, and he has written a very full account of it. Samuel Richardson came to Parson's Green in 1755 from North End. In Ashington Road stands the Church of the Holy Cross, a Roman Catholic building of plain yellow brick, with a cross at each end, built in 1886. Just after [Pg 69] leaving Parson's Green, there is on the right a high red-brick wall, which shows signs of age. Within it stood until recently Peterborough House, the second of the name. The original Peterborough House stood on the site of one still older, known as Brightwells. It was the property of John Tarnworth, Privy Councillor to Queen Elizabeth, and he died here in 1569.

Sir Thomas Knolles afterwards owned it, and sold it in 1603 to Sir Thomas Smith, whose only daughter married the Hon. Thomas Carey. It was he who pulled down the old house and built a new one, calling it Villa Carey. Carey's daughter married Viscount Mordaunt, younger son of the Earl of Peterborough. The house recently demolished only dated from the beginning of the nineteenth century. Bowack describes the old house as a "very large square regular Pile, built of brick, and has a gallery all round it upon the roof." Building of red-brick mansions and small houses is being carried on vigorously all about here, and the face of the district has changed very rapidly.

Wandsworth Bridge Road runs across Townmead Road to the bridge. On the south of Townmead Road there is a small hospital for small-pox, built in 1876. Below it lies West Wharf. Eastward acres of market-gardens extend right up to the premises of the Imperial Gasworks. This part of the parish is called Sands End. Some [Pg 70] where about here a very ancient house, called Grove House, stood. Rocque marks it "The Grove" in 1757 and 1761. The house called Sandford Manor is still standing, and is very little changed from the small print of it given on the title-page of Faulkner's large edition. It is a small white house close to Stanley Bridge, and has been often spoken of as if it were included in Chelsea. Addison, who lived here, used to date his letters from Chelsea. Therefore the house has been more particularly described in the section devoted to Chelsea. The Manor of Sandford is first mentioned in 1403, when Henry, Earl of Northumberland, gave it to the Dean and Chapter of St. Martin-le-Grand in exchange for a house in Aldersgate Street. King Henry VIII. granted the collegiate church of St. Martin and endowments to Westminster. The Dean and Chapter of Westminster granted the manor to the King again in 1549. It was sold by Queen Mary to the Maynards, in whose family it remained till 1756.

We have now traversed Fulham from end to end, beginning at the north-east corner, and ending in the south-east corner close to Stanley Bridge. Fulham can boast with pride of one ancient mansion—the palace of the Bishops of London—and of one literary reminiscence—that of Richardson—worthy to rank, if not in the very first class, yet somewhere near it.

FULHAM DISTRICT.
Published by A. & C. Black, London.

[Pg 71]

PUTNEY

By J. C. Geikie.

The first mention made of Putney—styled "Putenhie" in the Conqueror's Domesday Book, and "Puttenheth" in all subsequent records—is in connection with the fishery and ferry which existed here at the time of the Conquest. In 1663 the fishery was held for the three best salmon caught in March, April, and May, but this rent was afterwards converted to a money value. At the sale of Sir Theodore Janssen's estates the fishery was let for £6 per annum. The rent was afterwards increased to £8, and a lease upon those terms expired in 1780. Since 1786 this fishery has been abandoned. Mention is also made that occasionally a porpoise was caught here, and, as a matter of fact, two watermen shot one here lately; but it was confiscated, and the men fined for discharging firearms on the river. The ferry at the time of the Conquest yielded 20s. a year to the Lord of the Manor, and Putney appears at all [Pg 72] times to have been a considerable thoroughfare, as it was usual formerly for persons travelling from London to the West of England to come as far as this by water. In Elizabeth's reign it was ordered that watermen should pay a halfpenny for every stranger, and a farthing for every inhabitant of Putney, to the ferry-owner, or be fined 2s. 6d. In 1629 the Lord of the Manor received 15s. per year for the ferry.

In 1726, the twelfth year of George I.'s reign, an Act of Parliament was passed for building a wooden bridge from Putney to Fulham, which was finished in the year 1729 at an expense of £23,975, and the ferry was bought up, those interested in it being paid proportionately. The plan for the bridge was drawn by the celebrated Mr. Cheselden, Surgeon of Chelsea Hospital. The bridge was 789 feet long and 24 feet wide, with openings for vessels to pass through, the largest of which, in the centre, was named Walpole's Lock, in honour of Sir Robert Walpole, who helped to procure the Act of Parliament to build the bridge. A toll of a halfpenny was charged foot-passengers, and on Sundays this was doubled, for the purpose of raising a fund of £62 a year, which was divided annually between the widows and children of poor watermen belonging to Putney and Fulham as a recompense to the fraternity, who were not allowed to ply on Sundays after the [Pg 73] building of the bridge. This bridge was purchased by the Corporation of London, and by them transferred to the Board of Works, who erected in the years 1884-1886 the present substantial stone bridge on the site formerly occupied by the aqueduct of the Chelsea Waterworks Company. The approaches on both sides have been greatly improved, and it is now toll-free.

The parish church of St. Mary's stands on the river-bank adjoining the bridge, and was originally built as a chapel of ease to Wimbledon, and, owing to absence of all records, the date of its erection cannot be ascertained, though it is certainly older than the church at Mortlake (1348), for Archbishop Winchelsea held a public ordination in it as far back as 1302. The stone tower is of more recent date, being probably not later than the middle of the fifteenth century. The church suffered greatly in the dreadful storm which happened in November, 1703. Facing south on its tower is a sundial with the appropriate motto, "Time and tide stay for no man."

Pepys makes frequent mention of Putney and the church, and his contemporary Evelyn also speaks of the village. This place maintained its suburban character until a few years ago, and it is not long since the High Street was represented as having one broad pavement lined with stately trees, and a kennel on either side, by means of [Pg 74] which the road was watered in summer. From the bridge westward the river has been embanked and a promenade built and lined with seats, and this is a favourite spot on warm summer evenings. At the far end of this broad road are the boat-houses of the London, Thames, Leander, and other well-known clubs, mostly of brick, with dressing-rooms upstairs and wide balconies giving fine views of the river. Some boat-building and oar-making also is to be found here, as this is the headquarters of London rowing, and noted for the Oxford and Cambridge Boat-race. This race was first rowed at Henley in 1829, next from Westminster to Putney in 1836, and that course was adhered to until 1851, when that from Putney to Mortlake was adopted, and this, save on three occasions—in the years 1846, 1856, 1863—has since been the battle-ground of the Universities.

After leaving the High Street at the bridge end, the way to the river-bank is down what was formerly Windsor Street, but is now known as part of the Lower Richmond Road; and here on the south side, covering the site of River Terrace, now torn down, and River Street, stood "the Palace," so called from its having been frequently honoured by the presence of royalty. It is described as having been a spacious red-brick mansion of the Elizabethan style of architecture, forming three sides of a square, with plate-glass [Pg 75] windows overlooking the river, and possessed of extensive gardens and pleasure-grounds. It was built within a courtyard, and approached by iron gates. It occupied the site of the ancient mansion of the Welbecks, and was erected by John Lacey, citizen and clothworker of London, in 1596. Queen Elizabeth honoured Lacey with her company more frequently than any of her subjects, and between the years 1579 and 1603 at least twelve or fourteen visits of hers to this house at Putney are recorded. The house is mentioned as the headquarters of Fairfax in 1647. In that year, when Charles I. was at Hampton Court, all the Parliamentary Generals were at Putney. Cromwell was at Mr. Bonhunt's, the site of which is not known; Ireton at Mr. Campion's (a school in the occupation of Rev. Mr. Adams when Lysons wrote, and now covered by Cromwell Place); Fleetwood was at Mr. Martin's; and the other officers at neighbouring mansions, of which at that time there seem to have been many. Councils were held in the church, seated round the Communion table, the officers afterwards listening to a sermon. Two days after the King escaped from Hampton the army quitted Putney, having been there some three months.

Facing the river near the Putney Steamboat Pier is a big hotel, the Star and Garter, for long a landmark at Putney, and recently re [Pg 76] built in all the splendour of red brick and gilt. Beyond this formerly stood a number of old houses—Clyde House, Riverside House, Thanet Lodge, Laburnum House, Windsor House, and Point House; these had tiled roofs and bay-windows, and formed a picturesque group. They have recently been replaced by large mansions, called Star and Garter, and University Mansions. In Spring Gardens was formerly a curious collection of the cottages of watermen and boatmen, but these have now vanished. The lane has been paved and the whole district altered.

West of this as far as the common many alterations have taken place in the last few years, and now the market-gardens and fields are covered with street after street of small two-storied cottages stretching in straight lines from the Lower Richmond Road to the river. The same applies to the district between here and the Upper Richmond Road as far west as the London boundary at Northumberland Terrace. Here stood until recently prolific gardens and orchards, but now the site is covered with streets arranged as closely as possible, and filled with a rather better style of dwellings than those to the northward.

Passing west, we come at length to the gateway of the Ranelagh Club at Barn Elms. From this entrance, with its large gates and porter's lodge, the private road runs over the Beverley [Pg 77] Brook, and, swerving to the west, enters the park proper. This manor was given by Athelstane to the Canons of St. Paul's, and is still held by them. The mansion of Barn Elms was formerly in the possession of Sir Francis Walsingham, and here in 1589 he entertained Queen Elizabeth. Pepys and Evelyn both make mention of this place in their diaries, and it was here that the duel was fought—January 16, 1678—between the Earl of Shrewsbury and the Duke of Buckingham. The meetings of the Kitcat Club were held here in a room specially built for the purpose by Jacob Tonson, the bookseller, who lived in a house formerly known as Queen Elizabeth's Dairy, and died there November 25, 1735. At present Ranelagh rivals Hurlingham as a social outdoor club, and the merits of the respective grounds are a matter of opinion.

On the Lower Common, standing out by themselves, are two old houses, Elm Lodge and West Lodge, in big gardens sliced off the common. The houses are fancifully painted, and half hidden behind a privet hedge and a row of elms. The common to the south is bare of bushes, but to the north there are still big clumps of gorse and brambles, with many straggling trees between. Putney Cemetery is on the common, and further west that of Barnes is seen. At the beginning of the Mill Hill Road is an old cottage hidden behind closely- [Pg 78] trimmed trees and a high hedge, the residence of the cattle gate-keeper, whose duty it was in former years to prevent the straying of animals from the parish of Barnes into that of Putney. The gate has been removed, but the place marks the London boundary, which follows the line of the big ditch due south across the Lower to the Upper Richmond Road.

On the south side of the Lower Common stands a long row of staring Queen Anne cottages, and at the east end of them the Church of All Saints, in the Early English style, erected in 1874, with schools close by. Hidden away behind the church is an old wooden farmhouse, the last of many that formerly dotted these fields.

Passing eastwards, the Upper Road leads to the Charlwood Road, and across the railway-bridge the new streets, Norroy and Chelverton Roads, have been made as far as the High Street through the grounds of The Lawn, an old house which stood next the Spotted Horse. To the west short roads have been pushed out into the market-gardens, and north, at the angle, stands the Quill Inn, behind which Quill Alley, a narrow paved passage skirting the backs of the houses, leads into a labyrinth of small streets set at all angles and of all degrees of respectability. There are many newly-built flats on either side of Quill Alley. Every foot of ground is taken up, and [Pg 79] from the Coopers' Arms to Gardeners' Lane the district is compact with small houses and shops. Here in Walker's Place, a square of old houses, with gardens in front, under the shadow of an enormous brewery, was formerly a little wooden tumbledown inn known as the Coat and Badge. This has been rebuilt; it was so called from the insignia of the actor Doggett's annual prize for Thames watermen. At the end of this lane stands an old hostelry, the Coopers' Arms, and at the end of Gardeners' Lane was another, the Bull and Star, also rebuilt recently. Gardeners' Lane leads through a closely built up settlement to the Whirlpool, and here the last remnant of the market-gardens is to be found.

In the High Street, which is fast altering its character, there are one or two old houses, but the greater number are modern. The Public Library, which is situate in Disraeli Road, leading off the High Street, was first established in 1887. It is only since 1899 that it has occupied its present building, which, with the site, was the gift of Sir George Newnes, Bart., M.P., and was opened by the late Lord Russell of Killowen, Lord Chief Justice of England.

To the east of the High Street the residential part of Putney is built up of new, clean streets, laid out on the market-gardens and orchards that till recently occupied most of this district. [Pg 80]

In Northfield Square stood several fine old houses, one of which, Fairfax House, made way for the Montserrat Road at its High Street end; and another, Grove House, said to originally have been a convent, and associated by tradition with the name of Oliver Cromwell, disappeared when the western end of Disraeli Road was made. The railway-station adjoining occupies the site of some very old houses, and in the railway-cutting the workmen came upon a sewer, in which were discovered some silver spoons of ancient date. A Baptist chapel in the Werter Road, Oxford Congregational Chapel in the Oxford Road, and Emanuel Church in the Upper Richmond Road, supply the religious needs of the neighbourhood.

Passing along the Putney Bridge Road from the High Street, Brewhouse Lane runs north to the waterside; on one side are rows of new shops, on the other a swimming-bath. This lane was formerly one of the principal landings for ferry passengers to Putney, but to-day is almost deserted. An engraving of Fulham by Preist in 1738 is evidently taken from the steps, and shows the bridge and Fulham Church. From this landing a fine view is to be had of Putney Bridge; upstream and downstream is seen the big iron lattice bridge that carries the District Railway over from Fulham on its way to Wimbledon. A soap-boiler's establishment with several smaller yards makes the [Pg 81] lane busy, but there are still a lot of small cottages—some very old—of a poor type, and rented for the most part by labourers.

Passing on, the almshouses founded by Sir Abraham Dawes are on the south side. He was a farmer of the Customs, an eminent loyalist of the reign of Charles II., and one of the richest commoners of the time. Originally built for twelve almsmen and almswomen, they have been latterly occupied entirely by women. The north side of the road is here substantially built up, and the Deodar, Florian, and Merivale Roads on the Cedars Estate are comparatively new. Two old houses, Cedar Lodge and Crest House, remain, with Park Lodge at the corner of the Atney Road, newly fronted, but below the grade of the road. To the railroad arch which spans the road are built on the north side a row of new cottages with shops opposite. Beyond the arch at the bend of the road, which is here narrowed by an old house encroaching on the footpath, is a fine old mansion, Moulinere House.

Returning whence we came, we pass up the High Street and come to Putney Hill, which forms a test of the endurance of cyclists.

At the base of Putney Hill stands The Pines, the residence of Swinburne the poet. Here, where modern villas have risen most recently, and stately trees fallen most rapidly, stood Lime [Pg 82] Grove, the seat of Lady St. Aubyn. This mansion derived its name from a grove of limes through which the road to the house formerly led; and it was here in 1737 that Edward Gibbon, the historian, was born. He was educated in Putney till his ninth year, when he was sent to a public school at Kingston. It was on Putney Hill that the following event occurred: When Cardinal Wolsey ceased to be the holder of the Great Seal of England, and, obeying the mandate of Henry VIII., quitted the Palace of Whitehall, he removed to his palace at Esher. Embarking at Whitehall Stairs, he went by water to Putney, and started up the hill, but was overtaken by one of the royal Chamberlains, Sir John Norris, who presented him with a ring as a token of a continuance of His Majesty's favour. Stow tells how Wolsey at once got off his mule unaided, and, kneeling down in the dirt on both knees, held up his hands for joy at the King's most comfortable message.

Passing up the hill, a few new streets are being pushed into the fields, which are, however, still continuous to the westward, the limit of building being apparently reached for a time in that direction, and, after a short climb past fine houses with spacious grounds and drives, we come to Putney Heath near the Green Man, a quaint little road-house of the last century; close by [Pg 83] it is the old cattle-pound. The heath, of some 400 acres, somewhat resembles that of Hampstead, and from the higher ground some excellent views are to be obtained, whilst the sandy hollows and surface are plentifully covered with heather, gorse, and brambles. On the northern side, facing the road which leads to Roehampton, are many fine houses—among others, Grantham House, the residence of Lady Grantham; Ashburton House; Exeter House, occupied by the second Marquis of Exeter, who, divorced from his Marchioness, wooed and won for his bride a country girl under the guise of an artist; Gifford House; and Dover House, the seat originally of Lord Dover, afterwards of Lord Clifden, and now the residence of J. Pierpont Morgan. To the west of the heath lie Putney Park and Roehampton. Putney Park—styled Mortlake Park in old memorials—was reserved to the Crown by Henry VIII. Charles I. granted the park to Richard, Earl of Pembroke, who here erected a splendid mansion, which soon after his decease was sold, together with the park, to Sir Thomas Dawes, by whom it was again disposed of to Christina, Countess of Devonshire, whom Charles II. visited at this place with the Queen-mother and the Royal Family.

Putney Heath is divided by the Portsmouth Road, which starts at the Green Man and meets [Pg 84] the Kingston Road at the foot of the hill in Putney Bottom, and facing this road are many fine houses, as well as the reservoirs of the Chelsea Water Company, from which water is conveyed to the Middlesex side of the Thames by pipes beneath the roadway of Putney Bridge.

To the south of the reservoirs is a fine new house Wildcroft, the residence of Sir George Newnes, Bart., which stands in the grounds of the old Fireproof House, lately pulled down. This house was erected in 1776 by David Hartley, son of the celebrated Dr. Hartley, to demonstrate the efficacy of his plan for securing buildings from fire. This plan consisted in thin sheets of iron and of copper being laid between floor and ceiling to prevent the ascent of heated air from the lower to the upper rooms. The lower part of this house was repeatedly set on fire in the presence, among others, of the King and Queen, the members of Parliament, the Lord Mayor, and the Aldermen. The House of Commons granted Hartley £2,500 in aid of the expenses incurred, and the Corporation erected in the grounds an obelisk—which can be plainly seen from the Kingston Road—recording the experiments of the grant. The heath was the scene of many duels, among others, in May, 1652, Lord Chandos and Colonel Compton fought with fatal issue, Compton being killed. In May, 1798, on a Sunday afternoon, William [Pg 85] Pitt, the Prime Minister, who lived in the Bowling-Green House close by, fought a bloodless battle with William Tierney, M.P.; and in September, 1809, an encounter took place between Lord Castlereagh and George Canning, when the latter was wounded in the thigh. This last duel was fought near the Admiralty semaphore erected in 1796, the site of which is indicated by the Telegraph Inn immediately behind Wildcroft. Across the corner of the green from the inn is Bristol House, which owes its name to the Bristol family, who possessed it till a few years ago, and which was for some two years the residence of Mrs. Siddons. A part of the estate has been built on; many handsome residences have been erected.

Next is a large mansion, Highlands, and west of it is the historical Bowling-Green House, a low, two-storied mansion painted white, with large windows, and the Pitt arms over the doorway. In this house, shaded by fine trees, with a beautiful prospect from the lawn, lived for some years William Pitt, the Prime Minister; and here, on June 23, 1806, he died. The house derives its name from the bowling-green formerly attached to it, and for more than sixty years (1690-1750) the most famous green in the neighbourhood of London. The house had large rooms for public breakfasts and assemblies, was a fashionable place of entertainment, and noted for "deep [Pg 86] play." South of this Bowling Green House is Scio, a charming residence, with beautiful lawns facing the main Kingston Road, in the Gothic style, and from here the flagstaff and windmill on the heath are noticed. Close by was the gallows in the olden time, and here it was that one of the last of the highwaymen—Jeremiah Abershaw hung in chains in 1795, after suffering the penalty of the law on Kingston Common, then the place of execution for Surrey. Being crossed by a main road, this dreary neighbourhood was formerly much frequented by footpads and highwaymen. Aubrey mentions the gallows near here, and adds that Roman urns are often found in the dry, gravelly ground.

Putney Heath merges into Wimbledon Common, a fine expanse of 1,000 acres of breezy upland. The headquarters of the National Rifle Association till 1889 were in the Windmill, a picturesque landmark seen from far and near; but owing to increasing danger and the enormous crowds that flocked to the camp it was removed to Bisley in Surrey. The Windmill was formerly a favourite resort of duellists. Some distance from the windmill is Cæsar's Well, the most historical spot on Wimbledon Common, and its water is said to possess medicinal properties. This common and Putney Heath were in the last century the scene of frequent reviews. George III. reviewed the [Pg 87] Surrey volunteers here in 1799, as he had previously done the Guards in 1767; and Charles II., in 1684, also reviewed his forces on the heath. At the north-west corner of the heath lies the village of Roehampton, snugly nestling in a valley, and consisting of a small cluster of houses. The centre of the village is at the angle of Roehampton Lane, where a drinking-fountain, a gift of Mr. Lyne-Stephens, stands in the road, with the Catholic chapel of St. Joseph's, approached through a beautiful carved oaken lych-gate, facing it. This chapel and rectory stand in the grounds of Manresa House, a training college of the Jesuit Fathers. To the north is a quaint old village inn, the Montague Arms, flanked by a row of old cottages. Ponsonby Road and Medfield Street are lined with small houses, for the most part new, very clean, and well kept. The parochial schools, in two buildings, for boys and girls, are in the Ponsonby Road on the hillside, and between them is a church, completed in 1899. In the High Street, which is built up with small shops for a short distance, stands on the north side, well back from the road, the King's Head Inn, with its wonderful signboard displayed in the garden, its big, old-fashioned bay-windows, curious low-ceilinged rooms, and weather-boarded sides, shaded by great elms, giving it a very picturesque aspect. The gardens, with tables set [Pg 88] out in little nooks, and the stables of the house across the yard, complete a picture, of which few are to be found near London now. In this street is one of the buildings of St. Mary's Convent, a red-brick pile used as a laundry.

Returning to Roehampton Lane, and passing up the rise to the south, we come to the Alton Road, lined with good houses, and a little to the west the Bessborough Road falls into it, and runs through a favourite residential district built up with fine dwellings. Here the hollows made by gravel-digging on the edge of the heath are being, in a measure, filled up with earth from the building going on near by, and opposite The Elms, on the brow of the common, a peculiar tomblike building is noticed. This is merely a spring-house covering the artesian well that supplies the drinking-fountain in the village. At Highwood, a solidly-built mansion, we come to the Portsmouth Road, and after passing several villas, to Kingston Road at the foot of the hill. Here, on the west side, Richmond Park stretches parallel with the road, the enclosing wall being so close to the road as to give the houses hardly any garden; still, from here to the Robin Hood Gate there are many pretty villas, and at Beverley Brook a row of cottages has been erected close to the wall. On the east side of the road a new cemetery of the Putney Burial Board is under the [Pg 89] lee of the hill, and beyond are fields stretching southward, running up to and meeting Wimbledon Common. In the hollow adjoining the main road is the Newlands Farmhouse to which these acres belong, and adjoining is the Halfway House, at one time an inn said to have been the favourite drinking-place of the highwayman Abershaw. Stag Lane leads to the common, and further on Beverley Brook is crossed, here a narrow strip of Wimbledon Common meets the highroad. This stream from here, through the park, and across Barnes Common into the Thames, is the western boundary of London, and by following it we pass cottages on the right, and may note the beautiful views to the east toward Wimbledon and Combe. If we turn into Richmond Park through the Robin Hood Gate, so called from the roadside inn near, we come to one of the prettiest corners of the park, from which roads diverge in all directions. On the rise to the west is White Lodge, at one time the residence of the Duke and Duchess of Teck, parents of the Princess of Wales; and bearing to the right we see the deer-paddock, with Silver Hill and the King's Farm Lodge. The area of the park is a little over 2,015 acres, and it was formed by Charles I. in the early years of his reign out of wood and waste land. The wall—eleven miles in circumference—was built without consulting the owners and tenants of the houses [Pg 90] and farms enclosed. In 1649 this park was given to the City of London in perpetuity, but was handed back again to Charles II. on his restoration. The Princess Amelia closed the public rights of way through the demesne, but in 1758 a decision of the courts renewed this privilege.

Leaving the park on the right, we see Mount Clare, built in 1772 by George Clive, and named in honour of Claremont, the residence at Esher of his relative Lord Clive. On the west side of Priory Lane are three mansions, of which one, Clarence House, was for awhile the residence of the Duke of Clarence, afterwards William IV. Clarence Lane skirts the grounds of Grove House, which was in the reign of George IV. the residence of the celebrated danseuse, Mademoiselle Duvernay. The lane comes out into Roehampton Lane opposite Roehampton House, a fine red-brick building, with wings, erected in 1712. The ceiling of the saloon has a painting of the Banquet of the Gods by Sir James Thornhill, the father-in-law of Hogarth.

Southward, nearer to the park, are Cedar Court and Downshire House, two fine old mansions, the latter for a time the residence of the Marchioness of Downshire, and now a training college for army and navy students. At a bend in the road, where it goes downhill, is a quaint old-fashioned house, The Cottage, curiously built. To the west the [Pg 91] view is charming toward the park. Holy Trinity Church, now closed, was built in the middle of the nineteenth century, but the original church was consecrated by Archbishop Laud.

A very fine cedar stands in the churchyard, and on the north is the large and costly mausoleum of the Stephens family. Further north is the Convent of the Sacred Heart, standing in Roehampton Park, a spacious Gothic edifice, and opposite is the Rookery, alongside of which runs a lane through beautiful meadows past Putney House into Putney Park Lane. Towards Barnes, in Roehampton Lane, standing in wide grounds, are several family mansions, of which Lower Grove House, Subiaco Lodge, Ellenborough House, and Roehampton Lodge, are some of the best known. The new polo club, which it is prophesied by its originators will outshine Hurlingham and Ranelagh, has its grounds between Priory and Roehampton Lanes at their northern ends.

Roehampton Lane runs into Upper Richmond Road at its junction with Lower Richmond Road. Barnes Common, one of the prettiest of the bits of wild land near London, is rather cut up by the railroad. To the London boundary in the west, that is the Priests' Bridge over Beverley Brook, the road runs between hedges most of the way, but near the bridge are a few cottages and small shops. The Manor House stands at the [Pg 92] junction of the upper and lower roads, and wears an air of solidity, compared with its newer neighbours nearer town. It faces a small angle of lawn, backed by a hedge of rhododendrons, and is a plain, square, two-story dwelling with a porch, flanked by greenhouses; the walls are hidden behind ivy that climbs to the tiled roof. East of the Manor House rows of red-brick cottages on the north side stretch to Dyers Lane, and opposite is Putney Park Avenue, with its small cottages closely built; there are fields before Putney Park Lane which is lined with tall Scotch firs. Workmen digging here disclose the depth of fine sand and gravel which underlies all this region and gives it such perfect surface drainage. A gate marked "Private" leads into Putney Park Lane, and passing south under an avenue of magnificent elms, with the remains of orchards and market-gardens to the east and rolling fields to the west, we pass Putney Park House, and beyond a nurseryman's gardens see the Granard Presbyterian Church, a stone church with slated spire, standing at the corner of the lane that leads across the fields and past orchards and market-gardens to Howard's Lane. Westward from the church another lane leads through pleasant meadows, with beautiful views of the mansions that lie back from the roads, and comes out at the convent in Roehampton Lane. Towards [Pg 93] Putney Heath two large houses are seen—Granard Lodge in the Putney Park Lane, and Summerfield behind it. Passing down the lane from the church and entering Howard's Lane we find a district of new houses to the north, in straight rows at regular intervals, gauged, apparently, by the size of the backyards. To the south one row of small cottages, Upper Park Fields, juts out into the market-gardens, which, with the fields behind, are still free from buildings. At the western end of Howard's Lane is a large tennis-ground belonging to a local club, while beyond is seen the advance of bricks and mortar towards the west. Carmalt Gardens leads into the Upper Richmond Road at its best part, for all the houses here are of a good style and size. At the corner of Gwendolen Avenue stands a Wesleyan Methodist church of stone, with a square tower, and south a few houses flank it; but though all this land was lately open it is now built over. At the St. John's Road, however, buildings have rapidly risen, and the Church of St. John at the corner of the Ravenna Road is now surrounded by a well-built-up neighbourhood. Cambalt Road is also new, with strange types of houses, and behind this, again, is another avenue, Chartfield Road, filled with new houses, running through to Putney Hill. South of this rise the well-wooded grounds [Pg 94] of the large houses on the hill, with fields to the westward.

And thus we take leave of Putney, one of the pleasantest of the London suburbs, as well as the most accessible. The immense increase in the number of houses in late years testifies to its popularity; but there is still an almost unlimited extent of open ground which cannot be covered; and with wood and water, common and hill, there will always be an element of freshness and openness in Putney seldom to be obtained so near London.

PUTNEY DISTRICT.